"Lord, How Will You Get Me Out of This Mess?"

"Lord, How Will You Get Me Out of This Mess?"

KAY GOLBECK
with *IRENE BURK HARRELL*

Published by
√chosen books
Lincoln, Virginia 22078
Distributed by Word Books • Waco, Texas 76703

Unless otherwise indicated, scripture quotations are from the
King James version of the Bible.

For the protection of the privacy of individuals concerned, a
few names have been changed in this book.

Library of Congress Cataloging in Publication Data

Golbeck, Kay.
    "Lord, how will you get me out of this mess?"

    1. Golbeck, Kay. 2. Baptists—Canada—
Biography. 3. Arthritis—Biography. 4. Death,
Apparent. 5. Faith-cure. 6. Missionaries—
Canada—Biography. 7. City missions—Ontario—
Hamilton—Biography. 8. Hamilton, Ont.—Biography.
I. Harrell, Irene Burk, joint author. II. Title.
BX6495.G59A33   248'.2'0924 [B]   78-17395

ISBN 0-912376-34-1 (v. 1)

Dedicated to
the Glory of God
and to the faithful friends
who by their constant
prayers strengthened
and sustained me

Contents

Foreword

IT ALL BEGAN FOR ME one day in 1976 when my husband and I went to the PTL TV studios in Charlotte, North Carolina, to spend some time with Harold Hill with whom we were working on a book. Before we parted, Harold handed me two little cassette tapes. "Listen to these," he said, "and let me know what you think of them."

There was no big build-up, no electricity, no fanfare announcement, just matter-of-factness. Temporarily forgetting that Harold has a way of dropping the biggest bombs quietly, I received the tapes in the same way and tucked them in my purse. They might help to pass the time on our drive home that day.

But all matter-of-factness disappeared as we rode, enthralled by the gentle-voiced testimony of a Canadian woman named Kay Golbeck. We laughed, we wept, we held our breath. We marveled at the fantastic goodness of God toward His servant, the incredible things He had done

9

—and was still doing—in her life. I'd never heard a more unbelievable story—miracle after miracle—and yet I knew that every word of it was true. But more than that, Kay's account of God's power and His love were true not just for her but for all of us who could believe as she did. Oh, if we could only believe as Kay Golbeck had done, what might He do for us all!

I could hardly wait to get in touch with Kay to see if we might be of some help in getting her story before the world. One of the first things she said to me when we talked, and she kept saying it over and over during the months we worked together, was, "Give all the glory to Jesus."

When a first draft was finally submitted to Chosen Books, they had to reject it. "This isn't one book," they said, "it's at least three." I knew they were right. Kay's story was just too big to be believed in one book. We'd have to present it on the installment plan or people could never take it in. And each installment would have to give all the glory to Jesus.

Here, then, is the first part of the story of Kay Golbeck. When I last spoke to her over the telephone, I could hear her golden canary trilling ecstatically from his window-sill cage in her little house beside the big house at Singing Waters retreat near Orangeville, Ontario. And Kay herself was bubbling with rejoicing and enthusiasm. "The first phase of the work on our $250,000 addition to Singing Waters is nearly completed," she said. "And every nail has gone in with prayer and praise."

Prayer and praise have been constant accompaniments to our collaboration on this book, too. And it is my prayer —and Kay's—that you will read her story with such thanksgiving to Jesus that when you ask, "Lord, How Will You Get Me Out of This Mess?" your answers, too, will be so large they cannot be contained between the covers of a single book.

IRENE BURK HARRELL

Wilson, North Carolina
April 4, 1978

1

I Died

IT WAS THE SECOND MONDAY in October, our Canadian
Thanksgiving Day. As I lay in my bed in creaky old St. Joseph's Hospital in Toronto, I had much to be thankful for—
a God who loved me and friends who prayed for me. But
I hurt too much. And when the pain grew unbearable, I
prayed to die.

I had been hospitalized for nearly eight years, so ill that
the slightest vibration of my bed sent new paroxysms of unendurable pain through my wasted body.

Only sixty-two pounds of me remained. Though I was
only thirty-six I looked ninety. Most of my hair had fallen
out; I had no eyebrows, no fingernails. My voice came in a
barely audible whisper through locked jaws. My hands
looked more like bird claws than part of a human body. My
spine had so deteriorated I could not lie on my back. Not
one joint of me was movable; all were imprisoned in the
agonies of three different kinds of medically incurable arthritis.

13

For the last two years my "bed" had been a wooden frame topped with an unyielding thin mattress on which I lay face down, completely helpless, in the little room everybody except the hospital staff called "the dying room."

It was a stark room, designed well enough for its purpose. High on the drab gray walls were two gaunt windows, small-paned and uncurtained. There was my bed, a simple straight chair, a bedside table, and a crucifix on the wall. Nothing else.

There was room for another bed in the dying room and once or twice a month one would be rolled in for a few hours while its gray-visaged occupant began the long voyage to another room of the Father's house. A curtain would be drawn between us while a hospital priest administered last rites and weeping relatives stood around the bed as the patient gasped out his or her last breath. When it was finished, the sheet would be drawn up to cover the eyes whose light had gone out, and the bed would be rolled away. I'd be alone again to keep on dying. Surely God would be merciful to me and my journey wouldn't take too much longer.

I cast my eyes upward to peer at the mirror in the bottom of a toy periscope a friend had tied to the head of the bed in such a position that I could see it whether the nurses had my head turned to the left or to the right. Maybe I could catch a glimpse of a waving branch of a tree outside the high windows. But there was nothing. Just sky, blank and gray. A few times in the past I had seen a piece of the sliver of new moon through my periscope, and occasionally a star. But it was too early in the day for that. Too early, too, for the little family of mice that used to come creeping out of their hole in the corner at bedtime to sniff for crumbs around my table.

Every night, promptly at eight o'clock, when visiting hours were over, the furry gray creatures would make their little foray, pausing warily every few scampering steps to

14

sniff the air, their whiskers twitching in nervous expectation. Once, when the mice had finished cleaning up the floor crumbs, one intrepid adventurer climbed the wooden leg of my bedside table and leaped onto the space between the springs and my bed frame. I held my breath as I listened to him scuttering back and forth. What if he would decide to start gnawing on me! I couldn't have done a thing to stop him. The next day, I asked a nurse to stuff some papers in the space to spoil the mouse's landing platform. After that, I was free to enjoy my nightly floor show again, a performance illumined by two 500-watt light bulbs. They were kept burning night and day, summer and winter, in a heat cradle above my spine.

A global war was raging. Yet I knew nothing about it except for overheard comments and snatches of conversation. I was removed from the world, and no one thinks a dying person is interested in such things as today's news.

Sometime late that Thanksgiving afternoon, the nursing Sisters began to carry supper trays to patients along the hall. The increased noise and wafted aromas of food made me violently nauseated. A nurse was at my side almost as soon as I put a slight pressure on the call button under my hand. The empty retching went on and on.

In the days that followed, nothing would stay down. Even a little piece of ice on my lips would start the awful heaving, though every cell of my body was screaming with thirst. My prayers were inward screamings, too.

"Lord, please make me get well—or let me die!"

Intravenous feedings were begun and blood transfusions, each one more terrible than the last as doctors poked and probed to find veins to put the needles in. When they arrived with the ninth transfusion, I begged them not to do it. Every inch of my almost fleshless arms and legs was bruised, so sore I couldn't bear the thought of another needle. I longed to die and be through with all the agony forever.

15

But no one listened to me. I sobbed with pain and anguish as they did a cutdown on a vein in my ankle and went ahead with the transfusion. One of the nurses who had been so wonderful to me left the room, the streaming of her tears accompanying my racking, dry sobs.

And then, one day, suddenly, all the pain was gone from my body. And just as suddenly, so was I. What was the date? I didn't know. It might even have been November 20, my birthday. But where I was, dates didn't matter. For a brief moment, I looked down on the worn-out body of Kay Golbeck lying on a bed four or five feet below me. I could see the dreaded needles and tubes, the distraught doctors and nurses working frantically over my earthly body. It made me think of a discarded snakeskin, lying beside a woodspath in the spring. I didn't need my old body either.

Now I was lighter than air, floating joyously, moving freely. Without a trace of pain!

Where was I? I seemed to be on a path in the most beautiful garden imaginable, a garden whose very atmosphere was ineffable love. On each side of the path were glorious flowering shrubs, such as I had never seen before. Their exquisite fragrance filled the air, and I, who hadn't taken a single step in almost eight years, began to run through the wondrously brilliant light.

"Hello, darling!" a joyful voice called to me. It sounded like my earthly father, and I longed to stop and embrace him, but my feet wouldn't stop. They had to get into this wonderful place as far as they possibly could, without stopping for anything. I called out a greeting in the direction of his voice and threw him a kiss, confident we'd have the rest of eternity to spend together. My feet took me onward into such blessedness—the flowers, the gold and silver radiance of the place, my complete joy, the utter absence of pain . . .

But then Someone stopped me.

16

A mist appeared on the path a short distance in front of me, and there was a figure standing in the middle of it. I saw clearly only the hand held up before my eyes. It had a nail-print in it.

"Stop, Kay," a new Voice said. "You may go no further now. You must go back."

"Go back? Go back to that pain and helplessness?"

"Yes."

"Oh, no, Lord." I prostrated myself on the path in front of Him. "Please, Lord. Please let me stay."

"No." The Voice was infinitely gentle, infinitely authoritative. "You must go back, Kay, because I have work for you to do there."

I couldn't imagine how I could do any work imprisoned in the wretched body in room 27. Nevertheless, I saw there was no need to argue.

"Please, then," I sobbed. "If I must go back, I'll go. But may I have something to drink? I don't care about eating, but I've been so terribly thirsty—"

"Try buttermilk," He said. "You may drink buttermilk."

With that, the mist and the form in it were gone, and I forced myself to turn back the way I had come. Instantly, I was in the dying room again, looking down on the wasted body. I could see right through the wall of the room into the hallway. My mother and two sisters and brothers-in-law were there, and the snatches of words that drifted up from the mourners were planning my funeral.

"Don't cry, Mamma," I called out. "It's so wonderful to be out of all that misery. Don't cry, Mamma. It's all so beautiful." I felt that I was shouting the words, but no one paid any attention. Then there was the feeling of hot-water bottles being tucked around me; my arms, legs, and hands being massaged; and more needles being stuck in me. They hurt, and I knew that I was alive again.

2

"I Am the Resurrection and the Life . . . "

I WAS AWARE OF OPENING my eyes, moving my lips. A nursing Sister was bent over me, trying to understand what I was saying. After a while, she shook her head, straightened and strode to the hallway to call my mother. The look on Mamma's face as she came into the room told me she had come to hear my dying words. But the word I spoke over and over again, trying to make someone—anyone—hear me, was not a dying word. It was a living one, given to me by the Author of life Himself.

"Buttermilk. Buttermilk. Buttermilk . . ."

I must have whispered it a dozen times before Mamma finally understood the faint word, her ear almost touching my mouth.

"Buttermilk!" she cried. "I think Kay is asking for buttermilk!"

"Oh, we couldn't possibly give her that," the nursing Sister replied in horror. "Why, for days, she hasn't been able to hold even a little piece of ice on her tongue without retching. Surely we can't give her *buttermilk!* If she starts retching again, we'll lose her for good—"

But Mother would not be persuaded.

"This buttermilk may be the last thing Kay ever asks for in this world," she said. I'd never heard her sound more determined. "If you won't bring her some, I'll go out and get it myself."

A nurse was sent, and soon she returned with a small glass of buttermilk. I was too weak to suck it through a straw, and as the nurse held the glass to my mouth, she said, "Just wet your lips with it, Kay. Don't try to swallow any. You know we can't have you vomiting again."

I knew she meant well, but He had said, "You may drink buttermilk," and I *knew* I could take Him at His Word. My jaws were still locked, but with my neck arched, I took hold of the rim of the glass with my lips, and as the astonished nurse held it for me and tipped it higher and higher, I drank every drop.

And every drop of it stayed down.

For the next month and a half, I lived on buttermilk, and my dehydrated cells began to have their thirst assuaged.

When Dr. Gordon Ferrier, our family doctor who had been in Europe, returned to the hospital, he greeted me with a twinkle in his eye. He was well over six feet tall, a big-framed man, crowned with a rich brown mop of the curliest hair imaginable. His hazel eyes always looked like deep pools of compassion. Dr. Ferrier was the same age as my mother, and I had known and loved him as long as I could remember.

"Kay Golbeck," he said, "what kind of hijinks have you been up to while I've been gone?"

"What do you mean, Doctor?" I asked him as innocently as I could.

19

"I read on the books that at 3:05 A.M., on November 20, 1943, one Kay Golbeck died and came back to life again. What's this all about?"

I lacked the courage to tell him *all* about it, so I said simply, "Well, Dr. Ferrier, I *did* die, but the Lord sent me back." He seemed to understand that much.

"And then they tell me you've been living on buttermilk," he said.

I just smiled.

"You know, I don't understand why those fellows didn't start you on buttermilk the day your stomach began acting up. The calcium that forms the spurs around your joints in arthritis draws from digestive juices. Buttermilk is the best thing we have found to put the calcium back in the digestive system so it can function properly."

I smiled again, praising God for knowing everything and for prescribing just the right "medicine" for me.

What exciting new things I had just learned about God! Not just that He is a great and perfect Physician, but that just as He is with me in this life on earth, so He was with me in the life beyond. I had experienced for myself that death could not separate me from the love of God which is in Christ Jesus my Lord. Knowing that with such certainty, I was set free forever from all fear of death.

Dying had been a wonderful experience for me, but living again—even *with* buttermilk—was a tortured, pain-racked ordeal. Still, there was a brighter hope than there had ever been before. Our blessed Lord had said, "You must go back, because I have work for you to do." Surely if I was to do a work for Him, He was going to make me well.

"But how, Lord? And when? On this sphere of earth— or in some heavenly hereafter?"

Most of the time, in the long years of my illness, I had

believed that He was going to heal me while I was still living on the earth. Wasn't there proof in the top drawer of my nightstand: a little red notebook with its lists of earthly places I was going to visit and things I was going to do when the Lord raised me up? Such hope in the face of a physical condition that seemed to be heading irrevocably in the wrong direction *had* to be God's special gift to me, to keep me going until His plan could be worked out.

I spent many hours puzzling over His plan, pondering again and again, with renewed expectation, *how* He was going to make me well.

I knew it was customary to pray for the sick in churches at weekly prayer meetings, but the prayers were always perfunctory, "Lord, if it be Thy will, restore so and so to health, or give him the grace to bear his pain in the time of his affliction." I was sure I wasn't the only one who had never expected anything to happen as a result of those prayers, and nothing ever did. It had never occurred to me that the *really* sick could be made well through prayer. I'd never heard of it happening to anyone I knew. People in the Unity Movement and Christian Scientists sometimes reported healings, and I had a whole roomful of literature they had sent me, but I couldn't get any meaning out of it.

One day one of the nursing Sisters had come into my room and said, "You have so many wonderful friends, Kay Golbeck. Why don't you get some of them to carry you down to St. Anne de Beaupre? That's a Catholic shrine— like Lourdes—where many people have been healed. Maybe the Lord would grant you a miracle there."

I had thought about it a little but decided that if the Lord wanted to grant me a miracle, He could do it right where I was.

Many other people tried to help, telling me of other shrines where people had been healed, and sending me Christian literature and handkerchiefs that had been prayed over by some person said to have the "gift of healing." All these things hinted of superstition, hysteria, and exclusiveness, I thought, and I wanted no part of them. But the promises of the Bible were for everybody to read, and I wasn't turned off by them.

One day early in my illness, there had come to my mind a remembered fragment of scripture so preposterous in its promise that I could hardly believe it could be true:

> Is any sick among you? Let him call for the elders of the church; and let them pray over him, anointing him with oil in the name of the Lord. And the prayer of faith shall save the sick, and the Lord shall raise him up. (James 5:14–15a)

Hearing the promises of God, I had never been able to say, "Oh, isn't that wonderful!" All I could say inside me was, "Is that right? Does that promise really work now? Is it for everybody? Could I try it?"

I had insisted on proving the literal truth of many promises and, over the years, I'd learned through many experiences that God's promises were true, and that they were for me. But I'd never tested anything as remarkable as that scripture in James.

When a clergyman had come to my bedside early one day, I had besieged him with questions about it. He had sat close to my bed and leaned even closer to hear my weak whisper as I quoted my verses to him and asked, "What does that mean? What do you think would happen if we took those words seriously?"

While he had considered how to answer the first of my provoking questions, I had bombarded him with two more:

"Has anyone ever followed these instructions? Do you know anyone who would anoint *me* with oil?"

He had shaken his head, his lips making a thin line of exasperation at my naiveté. No, he'd never heard of anyone taking those words literally. Then he explained that the let-

ter of James was written to the scattered tribes of Israel, not
to twentieth-century Christians. Anointing with oil was an
ancient Hebrew rite, he said by way of further discouragement, and it had no meaning for us today. He was sorry to
disappoint me, but it was only for them.

"Oh, I can't believe that!" I had retorted. "We don't put
fences around any other part of the scripture. We don't say
salvation was only for them." I mentioned a few other
widely accepted promises of God, then threw a challenge
at him:

"How do you *know* this isn't for us? How do you *know*
it won't work for me?"

The poor man had looked dreadfully uncomfortable, as
if his clerical collar was suddenly two sizes too small.

"Please," I had begged him. "I can't get out to do my
own research just now. Won't you study about it some more
and come back to tell me what you find?"

He hadn't promised anything, just had shaken his head
again and shrugged. His shoulders drooping, he had made
his escape. I wasn't surprised that he never came back. But
I had never stopped thinking about that scripture. And I
had continued to ask everyone who came to see me what
they knew about it.

No one seemed to know very much, but the awareness
that those incredible verses were in the Bible had stayed
with me. And finally I was asking God the questions to
which people had given such unsatisfactory answers:

"Is that scripture still true today, Lord, or was it only for
people back in Bible times? And if it is for today, is it only
for very special saintly people, or would it work for an ordinary person like me? And if it is still true, and if it will work
for ordinary people, who will come to anoint me with oil so
I can get up and walk?"

I was aware of other scriptures about healing, too, verses
that seemed to promise what I had not experienced:

23

"I am the Lord that healeth thee" (Exodus 15:26); "Jesus Christ the same yesterday, and today, and forever" (Hebrews 13:8); and "With his stripes we are healed" (Isaiah 53:5).

All these began to blend into a symphony of expectant hope in my mind, and suddenly it was time for all my questions to be answered.

3

"Rise Up, My Love . . ."

WHEN LONG-TIME FRIENDS asked me what I wanted for Christmas that year, I told them, "Please don't give me anything that looks like a gift for somebody in bed." They had laughed and humored me by giving me a skirt and blouse. A nurse had hung the skirt and blouse in a corner of the dying room where I could see them.

Mamma burst into tears the day she walked in and saw them hanging there.

"Kay, whatever do you want with such things as that?" Her eyes filled, and I wanted to weep at the deepening dark circles of worry and hurt I saw there.

"Don't cry, Mamma," I said to her. "I have those things because I'm going to need them soon. One of these days, I'm going to get up out of bed and be well."

It had been my practice, at the beginning of each new year, to ask God to give me a promise, a special verse of scripture to serve as a prophetic theme for the year. He had done it for me on numerous occasions. And one morning early in January 1944, a wonderfully joyous verse reached my conscious mind and engraved itself there with indelible clarity:

Rise up, my love, my fair one, and come away. For lo, the winter is past, the rain is over and gone; the flowers appear on the earth; the time of the singing of birds is come; and the voice of the turtle is heard in our land. (Song of Solomon 2:10–12)

Through these verses, the Lord seemed to be telling me that the time *had* come for me to be healed. With such a certain word, all the hope that rested under the pain came vibrantly alive.

"Lord, if this is Your time, show me how."

A few days after the Lord quickened the "Rise up, my love" scripture to me, three letters arrived from three friends, widely scattered and unknown to one another. All said in effect, "Kay, I've a wonderful feeling this is the year when God will raise you up. I have given your name to a prayer group, and you can join your prayers with ours each morning at nine o'clock. I'm sending you a book I think you will find helpful."

The prayer groups were in different parts of North America—the Prairie Bible Institute in Alberta, a Bible Institute in California, and another prayer group in Boston. I hadn't written any of the three people in years. They could not have been aware of the desperate nature of my condition by any ordinary means. God's hand had to be in it.

When the first book arrived, I had to wait for a friend to come in and open it for me. The book was written by an English clergyman, a Dr. Cobb of Craighurst.

"Just read me the table of contents," I told my friend, holding my breath for what the book might contain. Every chapter dealt with some portion of the verses in James that had been running like an anthem through my mind. To everyone who came in, I'd say, "We'll talk in just a bit, but first, would you mind reading a little of that book to me?"

Dr. Cobb shared his own searchings about the scripture in James, his own initial doubts, and finally the amazing results as he experimented in his own parish with putting the scriptures into practice. Many of my questions were answered.

The second book, *Quiet Talks on Healing,* by S. D. Gordon, also dealt with the verse in James 5:14–15. More of my questions were answered.

Then the third book arrived, a volume by Dr. F. B. Meyer. I was not surprised that it also considered the same scriptures. Altogether, the three books built up such faith in me that I knew I was to proceed with simple obedience to God's Word. The promise in the Epistle of James *was* for today, and it was not just for special people; it was for everybody—even for me. If I would be obedient to God's Word, God would heal me. I would get up and walk.

There was only one question left: Who would anoint me with oil?

The Lord would provide the answer to that question in the fullness of time, I knew. Meanwhile, there were some other hurdles for me to overcome.

St. Joseph's was a Catholic hospital, and I had seen a number of Catholics anointed with oil in the rite of Extreme Unction, a last rite for the dying. The persons anointed invariably went ahead and died. They never got up and walked in newness of life. I believed I was not to die, but to live and declare the wonderful works of God.

And there was a further impediment, an old bugaboo that still lingered in me of wondering what people would think if I did something out of the ordinary. Deep down in me there remained some ridiculous pride that was not completely done away with until one day there came a little voice that said, "Aren't you being just plain stupid and foolish, Kay Golbeck? If the only thing that's keeping you tied to this bed and keeping you from being obedient to My Word is fear of what people will think—"

"Yes, Lord," I agreed with Him, the full force of my stupidity hitting me broadside. "I'm worse than stupid. Forgive me, Lord. I'll *bathe* in oil if You say so. I won't think anymore—ever—about what anyone will think about anything! I promise."

Then I settled down in earnest to praying that He would tell me who was to do the anointing.

Everybody's favorite nurse in the hospital was Claudine, a little blonde Baptist girl with striking blue eyes who was inclined to be a size or two larger than her rumpled uniforms. She made me think of the old Pennsylvania Dutch saying, "The hurrieder I go, the behinder I get." Claudine was so good to all the patients, always bringing the extra drink of water, plumping the pillows better than anybody else could do them, taking time for an extra-loving back rub, or a word of cheer. These extra ministrations kept her behind schedule in her work, and in hot water with her supervisors. Many a time, Claudine would come into my room, to stand behind the heat cradle and give way to tears for a scolding she had just received. There wasn't time for the tears to last long, and with her hair wisping out from under her cap, a spare tire of plumpness overlapping her belt, she'd do what she could to make me comfortable while I tried to console her about her own miseries.

"It's because you do so many extra things for everybody that you stay in trouble all the time," I told her. "If you weren't so agreeable—"

"It's all right," she'd say. "Someday I'll have my own nursing home, and there, the *patients* will come first, not stupid old routines that don't make anybody feel better."

And so I continued to ask special favors of Claudine. One morning God seemed to be telling me she was the one

28

who could find out about a minister who would anoint me. I asked her pointblank about it.

"Claudine, have you ever heard of any minister who would anoint a sick person with oil and pray for him to be healed supernaturally, through the prayer of faith?"

Claudine had been with me long enough to know I had some queer unBaptist notions about things, so she wasn't too surprised at my question.

"Why, no," she said, "I never have."

"Would you ask your pastor that question for me?" She agreed to do it.

"Be careful how you ask," I warned her. "Better not let on that you're trying to find out for someone who's seriously ill."

She looked at me rather strangely, but the next day, after she'd talked to her pastor, she understood my warning.

"He looked at me kind of peculiar when I talked to him," she said, "but he did give me the name of a Reverend Joseph McDermott, a Baptist pastor who had anointed somebody, he thought."

"Claudine, please telephone him and ask if he'll come to see me. Tell him I want to be anointed for healing." I was so excited, I could hardly speak.

Claudine made the call, and not too many days later, the mail brought a letter from Mr. McDermott. Claudine read it to me. Mr. McDermott said he would come to see me at his earliest opportunity. In the meantime, he was getting in touch with two elders who firmly believed that healing by the prayer of faith is for us today.

The letter went on to tell me what I should do to prepare myself:

We do not want to rush in without adequate preparation. I feel there is a great deal at stake in your case, and that great glory will come to God by the testimony you will give when He has healed you. Your faith will now be tested in declaring your intentions to be anointed for healing. Fix your mind on God and make no excuses for your act. Fear and pride and the dread of ridicule will be your great enemies here. You will have to get the victory right here before you can go on. You are departing from the traditional line of behavior. It will take courage. But we know by our attitude here whether we have faith in the healing ministry of Christ or not.

A few words of instruction:
1. Would you study Gordon's book as a means of preparing your mind.
2. Study the charge to believers (Mark 16:17–18); the Lord's command through James 5:13–20, with the bulwarking illustration of Elijah's healing of the Shunamite's son (II Kings 4); healings performed by Jesus; healings in Acts by Saint Paul, and the uses of prayer in the Epistles. Also ponder that the healing may be instantaneous or the seed of healing implanted so that the cure may be worked out gradually.
3. You should secure your physician's consent to your anointing. We need this so that I will be protected. If you should have a heart attack through the excitement, I would be liable for a legal action.
4. Search your own heart for sin in mind, thought, or deed, and confess and forsake all. Are you fully surrendered to God, placing your life without reserve in His hands?

Consider the case of Paul's thorn in the flesh. Can you master your doubt? If God can use you more in humility and suffering, can you say, "Yes, Lord"?

The withholding of healing is not a lack of power on God's part, nor a lack of faith in the patient, or the elders, nor is it proof that miracles cannot happen today in the church. It simply means that all rests in the holy will of the Lord, and in His wisdom He will ordain that which is best. If we are surrendered fully, healing or non-healing, it is the will of the Lord.

I am, yours in the Master's service,
Joseph McDermott

P.S. Some approach healing by the prayer of faith flippantly. The "I will try anything once" attitude is not of faith. We need that quiet assurance that this *is* the will of God for me.

What a wonderful letter it was! I had Claudine tape it to the head of my bed where I could look at it every day, reading it over and over again, being sure I had complied with every requirement a thousand times so that when the day came, nothing could be lacking in my preparation.

I knew I was fully surrendered to God, even there in the hospital, that He might use me in any way He chose. I had no other desire than that my life might be His completely. I spent a great deal of time examining my own heart, asking the Lord to bring to my conscious mind any forgotten sin or wrong attitude or resentment so that I might ask His forgiveness and cleansing. Even in those days, there was a lot of talk about resentment causing arthritis, and I wanted to be sure there was no resentment in me.

When Mr. McDermott arrived a few days later, he was a middle-aged man, his short torso not quite matching his broad shoulders—almost as if a weight had been put on his head to keep him from growing tall. He was glowingly optimistic and asked all sorts of questions about the doctor's diagnosis, the bright lights warming my back, the funny little rolled gauze "doughnuts" under my elbows to help prevent bedsores, and he even asked about the gap in my upper row of teeth where a tooth had been pulled to enable me to suck nourishment—mostly eggnogs—through a straw in spite of my locked jaws.

Mr. McDermott didn't sit down until he had examined every contraption about my bed, even bending down to lay his cheek on the bed to look at my periscope view of the sky. Under his continued questioning, I explained how three times a day the nurses would turn my head so that first one side of my face and then another was against the sheet. No, I wasn't allowed a pillow for my head, just a little one under one shoulder and the funny little doughnuts under my elbows and ankles.

While Mr. McDermott was satisfying his very human curiosity about these things, I lay there wondering if such a "natural" seeming man could be God's instrument for bringing me the miracle I needed.

"What about anointing with oil for healing?" I finally blurted. "Have you really done it? Have you ever seen it done? And if so, what happened?"

"Whoa, there! Slow down a minute," he laughed, settling back in his chair. "I'll tell you all about it."

I laughed too. I had waited this long. Surely I could wait long enough for him to catch his breath and answer one question at a time.

First of all, I learned that when Mr. McDermott was in his early teens, he had a very serious case of polio. The doctors holding no hope for his recovery, he had been anointed with oil and prayed for. Within a very short period of time, he was fully recovered and able to walk. In his ministry, he had anointed others with oil on several occasions.

"As a matter of fact," he said, "in this very same 'dying room,' I anointed a woman with oil in the name of the Lord, and she was healed."

I held my breath in expectancy.

"It happened a couple of years ago," he said. "She was a Mrs. Castator, an older woman with terminal cancer of the liver and other internal organs. She was scheduled for surgery, not because the doctors thought it would help, but because the family insisted that they try everything, even though she had lived a full life and was practically comatose already."

"You mean she got well? From terminal cancer?" I interrupted, hardly daring to believe it.

"Yes," he said. "The records would be right here in this hospital if you cared to see them. She had a lot of faith and was certain God would heal her. She sent for me a few days before her surgery was scheduled, but I was out of town and didn't get the message immediately. We anointed her with oil the night before her operation was to be performed, and—"

"*We?*" I had to interrupt again. "Who was *we?*"

"Two other men and I, men who believed in prayer and that Jesus is still able to heal today when we call upon Him in faith."

He continued with the telling, holding me so spellbound I *didn't* break in again.

"The next morning, when the operating room personnel came to her room to prepare her for surgery, they got the surprise of their lives. Old Mrs. Castator wasn't lying in bed where they expected to find her. She was sitting up in a chair, looking like she was ready to leave the room, all right, but on her own two feet. All of her jaundiced look was gone, and her vital signs were so good that instead of performing surgery, they took a few x-rays and sent her home the next day, perfectly well. God had answered that prayer 100 percent."

"Praise God!" I exclaimed.

"I have anointed other people, too," he said, "but never with results as dramatic as those in Mrs. Castator's case. And I anoint people only when they ask for it with faith. I'm not interested in playing games with God. Or in taking His promises lightly." He could see I was in agreement with him in that.

"How about it?" he asked me then. "Do you have the faith to believe God for your healing?"

I told him about some of the studying I'd done, the books I'd had read to me about healing, and how for years before my illness even, I'd been proving the promises of God to my

33

total satisfaction. I told him, too, how God had caused me to think seriously about the scripture in James for more than eight years.

"Yes, I have faith," I said, summing it up. "God's given me a *lot* of faith, but I know I'm still weak in faith compared to the faith He would like to impart to me. Maybe I need just a little more time still to pray and study, and time to let my friends know what we're thinking so they can be in prayer for me, too."

He thought that was a course of wisdom, and after prayer, the date was finally set for two weeks later, Saturday evening, May 6, 1944, at eight o'clock. Visitors would have left the hospital, and all would be quiet so we could concentrate on our task without distraction.

I let Claudine know the date and hour that were settled upon, so she could ask my friends to be in prayer for me at the time of the anointing service. Some of them wrote to me at once, assuring me of their support.

The letters were faith-building, and it was a good thing, because when my plan became known to the nursing staff, a storm of protest arose. The kind Sisters, who had waited on me so long and lovingly, tried to talk me out of this act of faith. Some were sure it would be sacrilegious for a Protestant to receive what they understood to be a Catholic sacrament. Several of them reminded me that I had been useful in praying for other patients. They were certain the anointing would hasten my death, and they didn't want to lose me. But I was not to be dissuaded.

Finally, the Reverend Mother herself came in to reason with me, expressing her fear that I would lose my faith if I went against the will of God in seeking to be healed this way. Respectfully, I suggested that if it were so, then I had been going against His will in all the years when I had submitted myself to the doctors who tried to help me, and when I had taken the medicines they prescribed for my condition. But she wasn't persuaded.

Neither was my mother. I learned later that for three months she had been carrying in her handbag the papers for signing me into what was known as the Home for Incurables on Dunn Avenue in Toronto. She didn't feel the anointing would kill me, but she believed I was hastening the day of my admission to the nursing home whose only exit was the grave. She wept and wept. When soft pleading didn't get her to stop making herself more and more miserable, I spoke sharply to her.

"Stop that, Mamma. Stop it this instant. I *am* going to be well. And you can do something to help me."

"What is it, Kay? You know I'd do anything, anything at all to help. I've so wished I could take your place in that bed—"

"I know, Mamma, I know. But you can't do that. What you *can* do is to bring me a pair of shoes and stockings from home. And my blue bathrobe. While I'm learning to walk again, I want something decent to wear up and down the halls of the hospital."

That triggered a new flood of tears. But they abated after a little while, and very reluctantly, she agreed to bring the items I wanted.

Dr. Ferrier was out of the country again, having left me in the care of Dr. Haulk, the chief medical man of the hospital. When I started to tell Dr. Haulk of my plans for the anointing, in order to get his permission, he refused to take me seriously.

"Oh, Miss Golbeck, don't be silly," he said. "We're doing all we can for you. This business about the oil and a lot of mumbo-jumbo prayer—that's not how people get well these days. Just hang on—don't go off the deep end on us. There may be a medical breakthrough in treatment of arthritis any time now."

When I began, "But Doctor—" he held up his hand to stop all further discussion on the subject. But I had to have the last word on it.

35

"Then it *is* all right with you," I said, not making a question of it. He didn't say no, just shrugged and grunted in disgust, apparently glad the subject was closed as far as he was concerned.

But there were others who dared to believe with me, praying friends whose expectations mirrored my own. What did I expect? I expected to be told to get up and walk, and I meant to do it. So convinced was I that the Lord would raise me up that on the morning of May 6, I asked the nurse to drape my blue bathrobe over the chair beside my bed and put my shoes and stockings close at hand.

That afternoon, I spent the hours thinking of the many things I had learned about God, and wondering what He would teach me in this new adventure of faith. He had brought me such a long way already . . .

4

Growing Pains

I HAD HURT FOR LONGER than I could remember. In the beginning, I had been dragged into this world backward, all battered and bruised. My mother, just turned sixteen, had nearly died in the suffering to give me birth. It took seventy-two hours for my painful and arduous journey from her warm womb cradle into the snowy rigors of a Canadian winter in full swing. Instead of squalling lustily and long, I had barely whimpered.

The grandmother who gave such good nursing care at my birth there in Toronto must have prayed the whole time, and it was surely the power of her prayers that kept me and my mother alive in the months that followed.

I was so tiny, Grandma's wedding ring could slide all the way to my shoulder, and a teacup was just the right size for a bonnet. They carried me around like a precious jewel on cotton batting atop a feather pillow so as not to add to my bruises. The neighbors didn't expect me to live.

Several years later, everyone's fears crescendoed when I

37

contracted scarlet fever. I can barely remember the fiery sore throat, my head bursting with pain, such weakness I could hardly raise my head for a drink of water, and unendurable aches everywhere. The curtains were drawn to keep my room dark, and a sheet dipped in turpentine was hung over the door to keep the scarlet fever contagion from spreading through the house.

Sometimes when people thought I was sleeping, I overheard snatches of conversation not meant for my ears:

"I doubt she'll make it—too frail," a well-meaning neighbor forewarned my mother.

Then it began to look as if I might survive the scarlet fever but be permanently disabled by its treacherous aftermath, rheumatic fever, which seriously affected my heart and painfully afflicted the joints of my arms and legs.

"The doctor says she'll never be able to go to school," I heard Mamma sigh to my father.

"Not go to school? That's what they think!" I fumed, glaring at the ceiling and gritting my teeth in dogged determination. "I'm going to do what other kids do if it kills me!"

And I did go to school, impelled by some inborn stubbornness that wouldn't bow to anything unless it had to.

There was an old white picket fence around the schoolyard just two blocks from the house where we were living in Toronto when I was eight years old. When I had struggled along that far every morning, I would reach out and pull myself from one picket to the next, all the way to the schoolhouse steps. It was hard sometimes, but a life that wasn't lived wasn't worth having, I told myself.

When I grew stronger, living—pain and all—meant sneaking out with my cousins and my sister Edith, who was two years younger than I, to engage in such forbidden "dangerous" activities as roller skating, playing ball, skipping, jumping rope, and going sledding, even though such strenuous activity was strictly against doctor's orders. My friends helped me keep my shenanigans secret. They'd never set up their games on the street where we lived, but always a few streets over, so my parents wouldn't catch me in the act.

But having to be sneaky about my athletic adventures didn't bother me much. There was only one thing that *really* bothered me: I was certain nobody loved me.

I didn't blame them, really. There was nothing lovely or lovable about me as far as I could see. I thought my nose too pronounced for my other features; my dark hair was so fine it always looked like an unruly cloud hovering around my pale face; and the big brown eyes people always remarked about because they were so like my mother's, seemed ridiculously large for the rest of me.

One Saturday morning when I was about ten years old, I was on my hands and knees under the dining-room table, poking the corner of my dustrag into the deep carvings on the fat legs. Mamma was sitting in a rocker in the corner of the room with my new baby sister, Florence, in her lap. She was hugging her and kissing her hair.

"Oh," I yearned as I peeked at them from under the edge of the spidery lace tablecloth, "I would just die right on the spot if Mamma ever put her arms around me like that."

I was never satisfied with the love that was shown in buying me a new pair of shoes. I longed for the kind of love that would hug me close and say out loud, "Kay, I love you."

Most of the time, I felt I wasn't really part of my own family. After all, anybody could see I didn't look like the other children. Edith's blonde hair and blue eyes were *so* bright and pretty compared to my drab brown ones. The baby had pretty blonde hair and blue eyes, too. I just *knew* my parents couldn't love me as they did the others. I didn't realize that these self-centered feelings were an almost universal part of growing up.

I never acknowledged my feelings, of course. That would

39

have hurt more than my aching arms and legs, and I was already learning not to complain about them. When I forgot, and mentioned my physical distress, my cousins teased me unmercifully about what they called my "growling pains."

"You're just like Great Granny with her rheumatiz," they'd taunt. "Bet you'll spend thirty-seven years in a wheelchair just like she did."

The awful aching in my limbs made wheelchair prospects seem much too real sometimes. Many nights I cried myself to sleep, putting a pillow over my head so no one would hear me. Father understood better than anyone, and sometimes in the middle of the night, he would come softly into the room.

"Where is it hurting now, my Katherine?" he would whisper.

"My knees, oh my knees," I would sob out to him, taut with pain. He would cup his big hands over my bony knees and hold them there. While the warmth suffused my joints with a kind of ease, he would tell me stories until I fell asleep. Strangely, I didn't recognize his actions as love.

During those growing-up years, I enjoyed going to school on Sunday as well as during the week. There were morning services in our own Anglican church, afternoon Sunday school at the Methodist church, and when Mother would let me, I went to evening services in the Salvation Army citadel, as they called it. That was another thing my cousins used to tease me about.

"You've followed the Salvation Army band so much, you'll wind up wearing one of those crazy bonnets yourself some day," they chided.

Even when I was nothing more than a toddler, I used to crawl through the bottom of the gate across the front of the porch so I could chase after the Salvation Army parade. If my family missed me during one of these parades, they knew they had only to follow the music to find me. Father loved the hymns, too, and he used to play his guitar and teach the old songs to us children.

I loved music so much I used to sit on a short box in front of a straight chair and move my fingers precisely, pretending I was coaxing magnificent music from a concert grand. When I was twelve, father managed to scrape up enough money to buy a used piano and give me lessons for a whole year. No one ever had to remind me to practice.

There was a great depression in Canada from the early 1900's until almost 1914. Work was very hard to find. My father had been apprenticed to the carpetry trade when he came to Toronto, learning all the intricacies of weaving beautiful rugs in the Burroughs carpet factory. But when times got bad, people stopped buying rugs, so he was often out of a job. There was no such thing as unemployment insurance or welfare assistance in those days. If there had been, Father would have been too proud to accept them. But he was not too proud to do any kind of work.

When he learned that men were wanted to dig holes for the pilings for a new bridge across the Humber River, he applied for the job. It meant long hours of standing in icy water, doing backbreaking work, but he took it on. No one was surprised when he came down with a very serious attack of rheumatic fever. When he was finally well enough to work again, he was limited in his employment possibilities on account of the permanent heart damage.

But there was always enough food, and we never went hungry. Mamma was a master of ingenuity, improvising and "making do" where someone less imaginative would have given up in despair. Every fall, Grandma would bring us a great quantity of potatoes, carrots, turnips, and cabbage from her garden, to be put away where it was cool and dry so they would last a long time. There were a couple of barrels of apples, too, their crisp juiciness more than making up for some of the luxuries we lacked. Liver was cheap, bones were sometimes free, and so there was always something to season the soup pot. Occasionally, there were even cookies in the cookie jar.

On Sunday afternoons in the wintertime, Father would pull my sister Edith and me to the park in our little sleigh. We'd build a snow fort and have a grand snowball fight, Father throwing as many snowballs as anybody. When a new baby sister arrived and became old enough to go along, she got the seat of honor, and we "big girls" took turns pulling her.

In the summertime, we would take long walks in the park and along the sandy shore of Lake Ontario. Father never permitted us to go in the water, and on those happy summer days, none of us would have believed that the night would come when I would wade out into the water alone, not to play, but to take my life.

Once in a very wonderful while, when I was a bit older, Mamma would let me pack a lunch and meet Daddy when he got out of work at noon on Saturday. We would walk through High Park, past Grenadiere Pond, and sit down on the edge of the Humber to fish. It would be well after dark when we headed home, and I would have to struggle to keep up with him, my legs nearly folding up under me. But I'd be so happy to have been with my father, to have been fishing, to have seen the woods, heard the birds, and exclaimed over the first wild flowers of the season, that my weariness was a small matter.

Those were rare delights, perfect days. But as I grew older, such special times seemed few and far between. And my feeling intensified that I was not really a part of the family.

The painful awareness that I was "different" was accentuated by the fact that on summer holidays I never got to stay at home. Instead, I'd be packed off to Grandma's farm in the country, with the explanation that the country air and all the fresh fruit and vegetables would help put some meat on my bones. I hated to go, and proved it repeatedly by losing weight instead of gaining any, but no one seemed to notice that. I remember spending many hours up in the apple tree where no one would hear me crying my eyes out from homesickness. I pretended that I retreated to my leafy hideaway to be out of earshot of Grandma's constant nagging of Grandpa.

Edith spent some summers at the farm, too, but she was allowed to tromp the fields after Grandpa. Seeing her happily garbed in a cut-down pair of his blue and white striped overalls, I yearned to follow them, but was told it was my job to stay at the house to help Grandma.

Every day, Grandma made me polish her colorful coal-oil lamps, trim their wicks, fill them with oil, and arrange them on the shelf over the dry sink. There were fourteen of them and it was a tedious task, but at dusk I loved to watch Grandma pick up each gleaming lamp in turn and light it. One lamp was set to burn brightly in the middle of the kitchen table, two went to the sitting room, and the others were turned low and put back on the shelf ready to be carried up later to the bedrooms. That part was fun for me, but oh how I detested washing their greasy, sooty chimneys every morning.

And washday was even busier. Every Monday, I'd help Grandma drag out the big copper wash boiler and put it on the woodstove, then carry kettle after kettle of water to fill it from the pump. While the water was coming to a boil, we'd be scrubbing the clothes with homemade lye soap on a bumpy washboard, making my knuckles so sore they'd bleed. Then the clothes would be boiled, rinsed, and finally blued and starched.

Grandma made her own underwear, fine cotton chemises with wide crocheted lace, ankle-length petticoats with heavily embroidered flounces. One day I expressed my disgruntlement at all the chores by starching her petticoats and her dainty handkerchiefs so stiff they could stand alone. But when she discovered my mischief, I paid for it. She hauled me back in to rinse the starch out and to iron them all over again.

The interminable ironing was done on the same day the stove was fired up for the week's baking. The little black irons were set on the back of the stove until they sizzled when I touched them with a licked finger. The handles were so hot, I had to hold them with a thick pad to keep from being blistered.

Looking back, I can see that all the work was necessary to make life go on, but the rebellious spirit in me made me think it was all invented to make my life miserable. I hadn't the slightest premonition that the day was soon coming when doing such simple tasks would have given me great joy and fulfillment.

5

"I Love You"

I WAS ALWAYS GLAD when it was time to leave Grandma and go back to town to start the new school year. But when I turned sixteen, I realized that I would have to drop out and look for a job instead. My father's rheumatic heart condition meant he wouldn't be able to support the family much longer. I would need to get some work experience and bring in some income.

When I learned that the Goodyear Tire and Rubber Company had a vacancy on its stenographic staff, I walked past the place day after day, trying to muster up the courage to go in and fill out an application for the job. I finally compromised by making my application by letter.

I had the essential qualifications for the job and could begin work right away, on a trial basis. One special instruction was given to me—I should put my flyaway cloud of dark curly hair in a bun so as to look properly dignified for the position.

When my first payday arrived, I grabbed my envelope

and, forgetting the pain in my legs, ran all the way home, hairpins flying in all directions. Breathless, I handed the envelope to Mamma, who counted the ten dollars for my first week at work. We were rich!

After I had worked for about a year, I met Alec, a tall good-looking persistent young man, who insisted that I go with him to the small church he attended. I declined, being quite satisfied with my spiritual condition. As a teenager, I had persuaded myself that being confirmed and saying prayers was enough religion for anybody, so I had stopped going to Sunday school and church altogether. But I still said my "Now I lay me down to sleep" prayer every night just as regularly and ritualistically as I washed my face and brushed my teeth. I even added a P.S.—"God bless Mamma and Daddy and the rest of my family and friends"—but I had no idea that any ears heard the prayer except my own. And no one ever answered. At least, I never heard any answer.

Still, I was almost superstitious about those bedtime prayers. I wouldn't have dared to get into bed without kneeling for the nightly recital. It was part of the prescribed ritual, and if I left out any step of it, something awful might happen.

"Aw, come on, Kay," my friend continued to pester me. "Let's go to the youth meeting tonight. What are you afraid of?"

The question made me bristle. But I didn't have an answer for it.

"Come on. It won't really hurt you to go, just this once."

"Well, all right," I grudgingly agreed, some unnamed force in me for once overruling my stubbornness. Besides, I liked the boy. "I'll go with you, just this once, if you'll promise you'll never nag me again about going to your church."

"I promise."

Thinking a single visit would settle the matter once and

46

for all, I walked with him to the little Baptist mission church in the frame building where other friends and neighbors had already gathered. That night I heard about a grasping, ungrateful prodigal son and the wonderful forgiving love of a heavenly Father. The tall dark-eyed young preacher didn't have to tell me that in spite of my leaving school to "help" my family, my heart was a prodigal. I knew it, and I was overcome with the enormity of my sin of ignoring God and running my life just to suit my own selfish desires. As I sat in the midst of the little congregation, I started to cry. Strangely, I felt no embarrassment, and I didn't try to stop my tears. They seemed necessary somehow, as if they had a cleansing purpose.

When the service was over, the Reverend Gordon B. Crofoot walked back to where I was sitting and put his hand on my shoulder. He told me to stay for a moment while the others went downstairs for refreshments and singing.

"Why are you crying?" he asked, sitting down beside me. His deep baritone voice echoed with compassion.

"You said God loves all of us," I sniffed through my tears, "and that means God loves me! I can't get over it. I've never thought anybody really loved me—because I wasn't good enough. But you make it sound like God loves me anyway—just like I am. That's so wonderful—"

His generous mouth broadened in a wide smile, and I burst out with new sobbing. When it had subsided, he handed me a fresh white handkerchief from his hip pocket. Then he led me in a simple prayer of confession of my sins, asking for and receiving God's forgiveness, and inviting Jesus to take charge of my life. Though I've forgotten the exact words of the prayer, I can still hear myself saying over and over again in amazement, "It's so wonderful—God loves *me*."

All I wanted was to respond to that love by loving Him back, and to express that love by serving Him forever.

47

When I had looked around me in the little church, I had seen that the friends and neighbors I had noticed on entering seemed to be sitting there, taking all that marvelous love for granted. Why, God loved them! It was the most wonderful thing in all the world, and they had just sat there as if nothing had happened at all. That triggered the first spontaneous real prayer of my life, one that began at my toes and went right through the top of my head. Walking home alone, so in the clouds of God's glory that I forgot all about the young man who had nagged me into going to the meeting, I poured out an impassioned plea:

"Lord, please don't ever let *our* relationship get ordinary. I want to learn all about You!"

Had I suspected what I would have to go through to experience an extraordinary relationship with God, I might have backed away from such a dangerous prayer. But God didn't let me know everything at once. He showed me one step at a time.

I had prayed my last "Now I lay me down to sleep" prayer. My new prayer was, "Lord, thank You for waking me up to really live!" And such excitement permeated my whole being that I went to sleep saying, "Jesus loves me! In spite of all my sins of omission and commission, all my mistakes, all the things I wish were not in my life, Jesus loves me!"

Pain? Oh yes, it was still there, but I had no time to pay attention to such a negative thing as pain when there was so much living to be done.

The new awareness of belonging to a heavenly Father who loved me so much, and the certainty that my whole life was His, just had to mean that I was to go to the uttermost part of the earth to serve Him. That, to me, meant I would have to go to India as a missionary.

For years I had been lured by books describing that exotic place of temple bells, open bazaars, sacred cows, and hypnotic dancers. It had always sounded *so* romantic. Besides, I knew several people who had gone to India as nurses or doctors after graduating from Toronto Bible College. I had no desire to be a nurse, but maybe I could be a Bible teacher. It was exciting to think that as a missionary in India, I could wear one of those lovely saris—

But first I would have to prepare myself for mission work. Since I couldn't afford to quit my job, I'd enroll in night school to finish my high school education, and then go to Bible college.

The first problem of my new life arose when, after much prayer and study of the scriptures, I saw that if I really intended to follow Jesus, I needed to be baptized by immersion.

I made the announcement to my family one night after supper:

"God's Word has made it plain to me that I am to be baptized."

I had written down a whole list of scripture references to back up my position, but nobody would look at them. Instead, they erupted in a storm of vehement objections:

"But you were christened as a baby!"

"You've even been confirmed!"

"Who's been teaching you such nonsense?"

I fled the table in tears. The next day my grandmother handed me a note:

"You were named Katherine after me," I read, "but if you go through with this blasphemous act, you're no granddaughter of mine. You'll be selling your soul to the devil, and you might just as well pack your bags for hell, because that's where you'll be headed." Her letter ended with a promise that she would never speak to me again as long as she lived. Since she and my grandfather, who had had a stroke, were living with us at the time, I believed I would have to leave home if I followed through with my intention.

I didn't know where I would go. I had no money saved. Almost all of my pay every week had gone to the support of the family.

I explained my predicament to Reverend Crofoot one Sunday after the morning service.

"I believe I have to be obedient to God's Word even if it means going against my parents' wishes," I told him. The thought of my packed suitcases standing beside my bed stirred up waves of distress in me. I loved my parents; I wanted them to love me, but—

"Wait a minute, now," Reverend Crofoot said. "Let me talk to your father before you do anything rash."

"Father won't listen," I warned him. "He hasn't gone to church much, but he keeps the Ten Commandments, and he has opinions about these things. Mamma and Grandma —well, there's even less use in talking to them."

"I know," he said, "but I doubt that your father will throw me out without a hearing."

Reverend Crofoot went to see my father while I stayed on my knees at the church. After a long time, he returned and helped me to my feet.

"Kay, your father has reconsidered his stand," he said.

I could hardly wait to see him. When I burst into the living room, I threw myself down on my knees beside his chair.

"I've been sorry to hurt you, Father. But I've been studying the Bible and praying about all this for more than a year now, and God has me fully persuaded that this is His way for me."

He didn't look joyful, but he didn't look angry either, and his voice was gentle as he said, "It's all right, Daughter. It's all right."

When I looked at Mamma, she only nodded and said, "You will do as your father says." Grandma kept her promise never to speak to me again, but she needed my help with Grandpa and we reached a kind of silent truce about it all.

The baptistry in the little church was brand-new, and no one had yet been baptized in it. When Father discovered that the water was going to be cold, he carried steaming kettles from the house and poured them in the tank to break the chill for me.

But not everyone showed such loving concern at the strange new goings-on in my life. Teasing about my dedication to the Lord increased:

"You might just as well take your bed to the church and sleep there," my sister Edith needled me.

"Hear you went swimming at the church the other day with all your clothes on, Kay," a cousin taunted.

"Yeah, she wore her clothes to keep from getting wet," a neighborhood boy snickered.

In a way, these things hurt me, but in another way they seemed not to touch me at all. I sensed it was all part of God's preparing me for the work He had for me as a missionary in a land where few knew Him. The old super-sensitive Kay Golbeck would have to die if I was to be really under the Lord's control. He was bringing me more and more to a place of utter dependence on Him and His love, a freedom from being controlled by what anyone said or thought. I could not have imagined that was later going to be a matter of life or death for me. I only knew it seemed terribly important at the time.

6

My Last Temper Tantrum

To my sister Edith I had always been impulsive, impetuous, stubborn, and bad-tempered. That I should now be trying to live a godly life bothered her. She was greatly relieved when I proved to be such a dismal failure in all my efforts at "goodness."

For I was far from experiencing the new creaturehood that God had promised me in His Word. I kept affirming with my lips, "I can do all things through Christ who strengthens me," but I didn't see the evidence of it in my life. I was still a daydreamer, a bossy big sister, a sharp-tongued young woman with, paradoxically, a shyness before the outside world that was actually painful to me. Where was the freedom from self that I was supposed to have in Jesus? It seemed sometimes that the rich benefits of belonging to Him were for others, and not for me.

For one thing, I had long had an awful temper. I wouldn't get mad easily, but I would let things that bothered me smolder and smolder and smolder until suddenly, BANG!

I would burst out in a blind rage. Later, I wouldn't always remember what I had done during my fit of temper. That was bad—but it was even worse when I *did* remember.

Still vivid in my memory was the shameful day when I had become positively infuriated during a girls' softball game. I was the catcher, and I didn't like the way the pitcher was throwing the ball. She was a show-off. Our differences grew more pronounced as the game progressed. Her fast curves were hard to hit and harder for me to catch.

When a particularly wild pitch socked into the pocket of my glove, I had had enough. Dropping my glove and the ball to the ground, I strode out to the pitcher's mound, my teeth gritted together, my eyes blazing fire. Before anyone could realize what I was up to, I had literally picked her up off the ground—the adrenalin of my rage making me more than a match for her far larger frame—and slung her into the dust while a gasp went up from the onlookers.

It was days before I could summon up the courage to apologize to her.

"What's wrong with me?" I wept alone in my room. "Why, Lord, do I flare up more often now than before my commitment to You?" I spent hours praying and weeping in deep contrition and repentance over my temper and other sins stemming from my wanting to have my own way about everything.

When I mentioned my temper tantrums to several mature Christian women, one said she handled her anger by getting a scrubbing brush and scrubbing the floor, no matter if the temper struck when she had on her best Sunday dress and bonnet. Another said she made herself whistle until the anger passed. Still another relied on the time-tested counting to ten. I tried all of these remedies, tried walking away from the anger-producing situation, but it seemed that no psychological trick would work for me. I still got mad and I still acted like it. I knew I was the worst witness in our whole church because of my ungovernable displays of temper. When Jesus said He came to give us a life more abundant, that *had* to mean that He could help me get rid of my bad temper, impatience, and selfishness.

I knew that some people slept with a Bible under their pillows to keep away bad dreams, but I wasn't interested in that. I wanted to take the promises out of the book and see if they would work for me.

I read a wonderful story of a missionary in the heart of Africa who had the faith to pray for a wind-up phonograph to use in her ministry in a little native village. Shortly thereafter, a record player appeared on the dock, all ready for her to uncrate and use in her evangelistic work. "How wonderful!" I thought. "But she gave her whole life to the Lord, and He *has* to take care of her. But would He do the same thing for me, somebody not good at all?" I wondered if God could help me overcome my bad temper. Could I be a really new creature, with all the old things passed away?

A major crisis came one Saturday morning when I was in the kitchen at home. Edith was there with me.

In our family, there were always four lunches to be packed every day for school or for work. On the weekend, I would usually make a cake or cookies to be used during the week for dessert in the lunches. Edith, now fifteen, would make the pies. On that particular Saturday morning, I had put my cake in the oven while Edith was still fitting the top crusts onto her apple pies, crimping the edges between her fingers. Since my cake had to be baked at a higher temperature than her pies, Edith was going to have to wait for the cake to be finished before she could let the oven cool down for her baking.

While I was washing the dishes from my cake mixing, Edith began to needle me.

"I watched you throwing that cake together just any old way. You didn't cream the shortening and sugar nearly long enough. I bet if the cake had been for your precious church, you'd have done a better job than that. As it is, the cake probably won't be fit to eat."

"I hope it will," I said, biting my tongue to keep any sarcastic retort from coming out.

When her first dig provoked no ugly outward reaction from me, she started in on another tack.

"That was one awful mess your precious choir made trying to sing last Sunday. I wanted to cover my ears. What was the matter? And *your* voice? It really stood out from the rest. Sounded like a sick frog—"

I gritted my teeth and let that remark pass, too. But I could feel the pressure building up inside me. Edith's next remark added dangerous fuel to the flames:

"And all those little games you're forever playing with the little kids in church. You must think you're some kind of a Pied-Piper saint or something, with such a flock tagging around after you all the time." She paused to strike an angelic pose, one hand on her hip, the other holding a shiny pie pan above her head for a make-believe halo.

I swallowed hard and looked out the window.

There rushed through my mind all the frustration and abuse she'd inflicted on me in the last few weeks. I'd found my clean, freshly ironed blouses crumpled on the floor where she'd thrown them after trying unsuccessfully to get into them herself. My best hose would be missing, and I'd find she had worn them because her own had sprung a run. My white gloves would have spots, because she had "borrowed" them—

While all these grievances were grating in my head, Edith abandoned her saintly stance and bounced over to a position directly in front of the oven. She started jumping up and down, shaking the whole house. I knew she was trying to make my cake fall into a sodden failure.

"Please, Edith," I begged her. "If you have to jump, can't you go somewhere else?"

"Go somewhere else?" She raised her eyebrows at me as if

that was the most ridiculous suggestion she'd ever heard in all her life. "I'm waiting here to put my pies in the oven, stupid."

Blazing with a fury that had been under pressure far too long, I flew at her, my scant hundred pounds easily knocking her hundred and forty across the room. Edith slammed against the wall, then slid to a sitting position, her eyes wide with astonishment.

My mouth fell open in horror. Forgetting my cake, I fled to my room, locked the door, and sank to my knees, awed with fear at the awful power of my rage. Why, I might have killed Edith without even knowing what I was doing!

"Oh, Jesus," I cried, "You promised that in Your name we could have the victory over all our sins of the flesh. But I don't have any victory over mine. I'm so tired of this uncontrollable temper. O Lord, please take it away, all of it. Help me learn to rejoice when I'm taunted, reviled, persecuted, and when people do things to annoy me."

I'd prayed about my ungovernable temper many times, but never before had I been shocked into the realization that I might do something irrevocable and terrible in a blinding rage. I had no intention of leaving my room—ever—unless the Lord gave me complete victory.

He let me stay there for hours before I felt the release of His forgiveness and His certain cleansing of me from this particular unrighteousness in my life.

I was drained of all emotion when I finally came out of my room and went to find Edith and ask her forgiveness. A glance into the kitchen showed her pies, mouthwateringly browned, sitting on cooling racks in the middle of the table. My cake, all shriveled and sunken in its pan, didn't look fit to eat. It lay on the drainboard of the sink in the chaos of Edith's dirty dishes. I realized she had taken it from the oven too soon and put it there as a mute suggestion that it was fit only for the garbage pail. It looked as if the usual remedy for a fallen cake—putting an upside-down saucer under the bottom to bulge it up level—wouldn't work this time. But even knowing that, I felt no ugly reaction in me that Edith's gymnastics were responsible. I was able to smile. It was all right. A cake didn't matter all that much. Forgiveness, eternal life, and obedience to Jesus did.

I found Edith in the backyard, looking at a magazine. She didn't look up as I approached her, but I could tell she was listening. The Lord made it simple and easy for me.

"Edith," I said, "please forgive me for hurting you. I'm terribly sorry. With the Lord's help, I can promise that nothing like that will ever happen again. No matter what you say or do." She looked at me blankly, kind of shrugged her shoulders, and resumed her listless turning of the pages.

In the days that followed, there were a few little remarks designed to test me, but the Lord enabled me to brush them aside, with rejoicing in my heart for how He had healed me of any tendency to react against Edith in an explosive manner.

Have I ever been angry again? Oh, yes! But never at Edith.

It was wonderful, not having to smolder when she accused me of being "far out," or when she introduced me as the "nut of the family." And, in time, Edith became the most loving, supportive, helpful sister God ever made. Years later, she invited me to play the organ at her wedding.

But there were other tests of my "new creaturehood" that weren't so easy.

7

Prepared for a Disappointment

As a new Christian, I took very seriously the words, "Be ye doers of the word, and not hearers only, deceiving your own selves" (James 1:22). I was indeed being a doer of some things morning, noon, and night, and sometimes far into the night. I was always doing, doing, doing.

I was occupied with my secretarial work by day, attending school at night, being extremely active in church work and outreach to the community, but everything was going wrong.

I choked back a sob at the epidemic of tragedies that tore at my heart. First, a long-hoped-for baby brother—Ralph Clayton, named for my father—was born, and he died within a few days from a heart defect. A little more than a year later, a second baby brother, Harvey, arrived with hair like an almost-blonde angel. How I loved him! But then came the awful day when this sturdy 2½-year-old toddler was rushed to St. Joseph's hospital with a severe case of pneumonia. Mother had spent the night with him while I had gone home to see to the rest of the family, pack the lunches for school and work, and cook supper and breakfast the next morning. I had spent the night on my knees, praying that Harvey would recover, and I'd had such wonderful assurance that I could scarcely wait for the first streetcar in the morning to take me back to the hospital with the good news. When I left home, I cheerfully told my father and my sisters, "Now don't any of you worry about Harvey. He's going to be well!"

Getting off the streetcar a block from the hospital, I had almost run the rest of the way, flown up the stairs to the second floor, and down the hallway to room 27. Greeting my mother with a hug and a kiss, and wishing I could take the tiredness from her eyes, I whispered, so as not to wake my brother, "Don't worry, Mamma. Harvey's going to be all right."

She told me the orderlies would be coming for him in about twenty minutes. The doctors had decided to perform surgery to remove a couple of ribs so they could drain the fluid from his lungs.

At that moment, Harvey opened his great blue eyes, so like my father's. He called, "Mamma," and struggled to sit up. As she reached out her arms to support him, he gave a little smile, a tiny gasp of breath and was gone.

The sorrow-filled years swam together in a blur of tears— precious babies dying, the death of both my aging grandparents, and pneumonia cutting down my two best friends . . .

In the face of all the dying, my dream of going to India seemed remote, and I was dead inside, empty. My life was a great gaping void. The busy-busy-busy-ness didn't shut out the hurt. It only made the void bigger. Nothing could crowd out my acute awareness of that vast, aching emptiness. More than once I cried out, "Why, Lord? Why all this sorrow?" But instead of hearing a reassuring answer, I heard only the silence.

At the same time, my constant companion, pain, became more demanding than ever of my energy and attention.

The agony in my back and legs was constant, stemming from the arthritis that had set in after my childhood bout with rheumatic fever. So intense was the pain when I sat down for any length of time that I usually stood up and placed my shorthand pad on top of a filing cabinet while my boss dictated his letters. When he had finished, I'd retreat to my little cubicle of an office, where no one could see me, and kneel on a cushion on my typing chair while I prepared the letters. When my boss asked me why I didn't sit down to take dictation, I just laughed and said, "Oh, I sit down too much. It's restful to stand."

Even while I was standing, sometimes the pain would be excruciating, beginning in my sacroiliac and traversing a long and tortured route down the sciatic nerves into my feet. Other days, the back and leg pain was eclipsed by such awful aching in my arms that I thought they would drop off.

Even so, the worst hurt, always, was in my heart. But I didn't tell anyone about any of these pains because I had grown up in the discipline that people must be strong, and not betray their inner feelings. After all, my parents had reasoned, life was hard for everybody, and the rest of the world preferred to live without being subjected to the catalog of others' personal miseries. And so I continued to bottle my miseries up inside myself.

Many times my despair led me to a lonely rock on the shore of Lake Ontario when it was dark and stormy and no one could hear my cries. When that retreat was not possible because of weakness and pain, I did what I had done as a child—I buried my head under my pillow to muffle my sobs. But Father no longer came in to comfort me.

While my faith struggled unceasingly to affirm over and over God's promise, "I will never leave thee nor forsake thee," the affirmation didn't reach the empty hole I carried instead of a heart. I reached the darkest of times, when it seemed I was separated even from God Himself. I suppose the blackness that engulfed me was akin to what the mystics call "the dark night of the soul." To me, it was a vivid illustration that just as we can experience the blessings of heaven in the here and now, so we can experience hell in the here and now, too. I felt so terribly alone.

On a night without stars or moon, bowed with soul sickness, I went plodding along the edge of the lake which seemed blacker than the sky. Blackest of all was the awful, ugly emptiness inside me, the void in my jam-packed life.

Determined to find some peace or to die, I succumbed to an overpowering urge and turned abruptly and headed out into the icy water. I waded in almost to my waist, aware that I could step into a hole and be over my head in a moment. There would be no one to hear me cry out, no one to rush to my rescue. And I would have neither the strength nor the inclination to struggle. I wouldn't care. It would be such a simple way to end the unendurable pain of living. I wouldn't even need to wait until I stepped into a hole accidentally. All I had to do was to fall forward on my face. In a few minutes, it would be finished.

Looking up at the black sky, I cried out, "O my Lord, forgive me. But I can't go on unless You take away this emptiness and satisfy my heart."

How long I was in that icy water, waiting, looking up into the blackness of closed heavens, I do not know. Time ceased to exist while my heart was hurling the challenge to Him to so fill the empty place in me that I would not ever again be dependent on any human relationship.

As I waited, every cell of me defiant, I got colder and wetter, and the water, sky, and the inside of me got blacker and blacker—

Then suddenly, instead of feeling the water lapping up around me on the outside, I was being flooded with water on the inside! All the black emptiness in me was being filled to overflowing with light! It was as if God had turned on a huge tap in the heavens, and a gush of living water was filling me. It lifted my feet and put them on the shore while tears of joy and wonder overflowed in such ecstatic profusion that I was as wet from my neck down as I had been from my feet up.

I cried, I laughed, I sang, I jumped for joy, such joy that for a few hours it all but obliterated awareness of the pain. Oh, the aching was still there, but it was as if it didn't matter. The pain didn't belong to me—the joy did. And there was no hurt at all in my heart.

The sky was still black, but it seemed no longer dark. There was a glowing radiance to the earth, the sky, and the water. And such a radiance in me! Hour after hour I danced up and down the shoreline, exulting, almost unaware of my feet touching the ground. A glorious Presence was within me, obliterating every trace of the emptiness, satisfying my heart completely.

I knew instinctively that I had just been filled with the Holy Spirit. It was Jesus, baptizing me with His own intimate presence. The windows of heaven were open, and God was pouring out blessing through their portals. The perfect Comforter had taken up residence in my heart. It was as if I had to be ready to die—in order to be equipped to live.

All this was so real to me that for months afterward, I couldn't sweep a floor, wash a dish, or make a bed without being conscious of the immediate presence of the One who fills all things.

"Oh, Jesus," I'd pray, as I tucked in a sheet or smoothed a blanket, "let the one who sleeps in this bed sleep peacefully. Let him be aware of Your presence in everything." Washing a cup, I'd say, "Dear Lord, thank You for being with me right now. Let whoever drinks from this cup be filled to overflowing with Your love."

My pulse beat as one with His pulse. There seemed to be no separation. I would laugh with the joy that we were functioning as one being.

And being so acutely, intensely aware of His presence and His love, I was surprisingly open to receive and to realize love for—and from—other people, too. For the first time in my life, I began to feel accepted and loved by my own family.

As long as I could remember, I had recited a creed that said, "And I believe in the Holy Ghost." I had given no particular thought to what those words meant, except for thinking they sounded a little spooky.

But that day, I knew something far beyond mere mental assent to the existence of such a Being as the Holy Ghost. I was experiencing Him for myself. The love of God was being shed abroad in my heart by the Holy Ghost, and it was altogether wonderful. He had come into me to lift up the reality of Jesus, to magnify and glorify His presence in my life, just as the scripture had said He would.

The rest of the nine years of working and going to school were full of hard work, illness, and pain—but they passed quickly because I was overflowing with the certain knowledge of the constant presence of Jesus with me. And I looked forward with longing to the day when I'd be sharing that presence with brown-skinned people who didn't yet know my Lord.

At the end of nine years, when classes were finished, I took my diploma and other credentials and marched down to the foreign mission board. The song in my heart was, "India, here I come!"

But the missionary board officials didn't just look at my papers and hand me a ticket for the next boat to India. It was far more complicated than that.

"The first thing you must do," they told me, "is to see the mission doctor for the necessary physical examination."

"Physical examination?" I sputtered. I hadn't dreamed that I would need to see a doctor once my other qualifications were in order.

"Oh, yes," they assured me. "We have to make sure you're healthy enough to withstand the hardships of missionary life."

"Well," I laughed, "I've been surviving Canadian winters for years now. India shouldn't be too much harder to handle than that." But it was with a gnawing uneasiness that I went to see the doctor. Would he guess I had done my stenographic work for the last three years standing up or kneeling because of the awful pain in my back?

The doctor's examination was brief, too brief. Just a stethoscope placed on my chest for a few minutes, then a question or two which I had to answer honestly. He didn't even bother to write my answers on the forms on his desk. Instead, his brimming steely-gray eyes looked out over his glasses as he put his stethoscope down on his desk.

"So you want to go to India, do you, Kay Golbeck?"

"Oh, yes sir," I responded eagerly. "I've got my trunk half-packed."

He shook his head, cleared his throat, and stared at me intently.

"Listen, young lady—" There was an awesome finality in his voice. "You can get someone to unpack the trunk, and you can just forget the whole thing. You're not fit to go anywhere, except maybe to a hospital."

"A hospital?" I didn't understand. "But I'm no sicker than I've ever been—"

I quickly covered my mouth to stop the telltale words. But it was useless. He knew, without my telling him.

"Just so," he nodded. "Just so. India, indeed. You'd better start taking care of yourself instead." He pulled a handkerchief from his pocket and honked noisily, then stood up to dismiss me.

64

"Where do you live? Let me call a cab to take you home."

"Oh, I can't afford a cab," I protested. "I live miles from here—but it's all right, I'm used to walking. But why can't I go to India? I've counted on it so—"

He answered without words, gesturing toward his stethoscope and running his fingers down the spinal column of the little skeleton on his desk. Then he cleared his throat again and spoke gruffly:

"You're in very serious condition, young lady, and I advise you to see your family doctor at the earliest possible moment. You have the most advanced case of . . ."

I didn't hear the rest of it.

The tears rolled down, hot and salty, as I shoved my way through the door, down the dim hallway, and out onto the sidewalk.

8

Mission Impossible

NOT GO TO INDIA? Not go to India? Did that mean I couldn't serve the God who loved me so much? Surely I would die if I couldn't show my love for Him. All the long way home, and for the next two days, I could think of nothing but my crushing disappointment. But then those rivers of living water, ceaselessly flowing inside me, reminded me that Jesus was still with me, and that He still had a plan for my life. Maybe an even better plan than the one I had dreamed up. That all *my* old dreams had to be wrapped up and put away didn't have to mean that there were no dreams left.

But what dreams, Lord? What is Your dream for me?

I had an inkling of the answer almost before the question was fully formed in my heart. Foreign missions required a physical examination I could not pass, but there was no physical required for home mission work. India wasn't the only place where people were hurting. I had already done quite a bit of volunteer work for some of the missions in the city of Toronto and its suburbs. I'd called on parishioners, visited the sick, taught classes—I'd seen that they had needs, desperate needs.

One day I had taken some Christmas gifts to a family where there was a new baby every year. When I arrived at the house, I had found the woman sitting in front of the oven door trying to get warm, weeping because there was no money to buy gifts for the children. As I put my arm around her, comforting her, something warned me to look over my shoulder. I saw her drunken husband with an upraised butcher knife, and a look of maniacal glee on his face. He was after *me!* I raced around the kitchen table, barely keeping out of reach, until the wife came to her senses long enough to stick out her foot and send her husband sprawling across the floor. The knife clattered out of sight under the icebox. That gave me the precious seconds I needed to get out of the house and run for help.

Undaunted by this narrow escape, I made my application to be a home missionary before word could spread about my physical condition, and the board placed my name on a list for the next opening. No one so much as mentioned a physical examination.

It took me less than a month to present my credentials, to be given a position among Polish immigrants, to break the news to my family, and to pack my suitcase for Hamilton, Ontario.

The day I left home, my mother knelt at my feet and begged me not to go. Edith was happily planning to be married, and I tried to reason with Mother.

"Mamma, if I were getting married, like Edith, you wouldn't feel this way about my leaving home."

"Of course not," she wailed. "And that's what *you* ought to be doing—getting married—not gallivanting off somewhere to work with foreigners you don't even know."

"But I'll get to know them, Mamma," I promised. "And this is the way God has chosen for my life just now. It's like being married, in a way—"

She only shook her head, and clung to me more tenaciously, until I was weeping along with her. It was only the strength of God that enabled me to break away and walk out the door.

"I have to go, Mamma. It's something I must do."

Later I had a letter from a friend who understood. He wrote,

> I know it must have been very hard to leave home, especially when your loved ones did not wish it, but remember that it may be a means of drawing many to the saving power of Jesus Christ. You have done the right thing. We are praying for you, remembering the words of the Lord Jesus, "He that loveth father or mother more than me is not worthy of me." (Matthew 10:37)

Oh, how I longed to be found worthy of Him.

My father drove me to the neat little red brick Baptist mission building in Hamilton that bitter, cold January Sunday. Leaving me there just in time for the afternoon Sunday School session, he took my suitcase and a box of books to the home of a friend who lived about a mile away. I was planning to stay with her only temporarily—until I could find suitable lodgings closer to the mission.

After the Sunday School service, during which I met the Sunday School teacher and the "faithful few," among them a handful of shivering children, I walked to my friend's house for supper, then fought my way back against the wind to the mission for the Polish service that night.

Meeting children had always been easy for me, but meeting their foreign-looking—and foreign-sounding—parents was terrifying. I was frightened almost to death at their

68

strangeness as they must have been at mine. And I wondered how it would ever be possible for us to get to know one another.

Months later, I learned that everyone thought I had come in looking like a lamb about to be slain, and they had felt so sorry for me, it had helped to break down the wall between us. But at the time, I saw only the wall, tall and thick, without a single toehold in it for climbing up.

The walk "home" after my first encounter with the people of the mission community was so long and cold, I resolved to move as soon as I could.

Every day as I walked, trudging through snowbanks, the icy wind threatening to blow me away, I kept my eyes open for closer lodgings. But there was nothing, nothing except the ramshackle deserted "parsonage" a block from the mission. I supposed I *could* live there—

"But Lord, I can't live in such a dirty, tumbledown place as that!"

There was no answer, just an awareness that my King had been born in a stable, and so I sought permission from the mission board to move in. It was my only alternative to fighting winter cold four extra miles a day on top of all the necessary outdoor walking the mission work required.

When I carried my suitcase into the big dirty gray frame house, there was one note of thanksgiving in me—at least my father didn't know the condition of the place where I would be living. He'd have told me to come home, and I might not have been too hard to persuade.

On my first night in the rickety old mission parsonage, I had to feel my way up to my second-floor rooms. The hallway light fixture lacked a bulb, and I was relieved to get inside my room, snap on a light, and shut the door. Undressing for bed was an eerie experience. Something rattled, creaked, or screeched every time I moved. And sometimes when I didn't. I'd never stayed all by myself before, except at home.

Shivering with fear and cold, I made up the bed with the sheets I had brought in my suitcase, piled the blankets on, and knelt to say my prayers before crawling in to try to get warm. The wind was doing its usual winter howling through the drifts outside. The whole place was so scary, I had to keep saying the twenty-third Psalm over and over to keep from dying with fright. Somehow, this wasn't exactly what I had visualized when I dreamed of being a missionary.

After a long time, I felt drowsy and was half asleep when I heard an awful CRASH! like a door being kicked open. Then a door slammed shut. Window panes rattled, and heavy footsteps began coming up the stairs, interspersed with thumps that sounded like a body lurching first against one stair wall and then another. A drunk!

"Lord, help me! Help me, please!" I prayed, sliding out of bed to pile the room's three chairs against the door. Hardly daring to breathe, I struggled to shove a chest of drawers over against them for further barricade, hoping my noise wouldn't be noticed by the intruder who was making so much noise of his own. "Lord, *please* look after me!" I kept praying.

The memory of my close escape from the maniac with the knife in Toronto was fresh, too fresh, and there was no one here to help me. My panic increased, hearing the heavy steps and the wall-bumping come closer and closer to my room. With one particularly loud bump, a picture fell from the wall and crashed loudly to the floor. Putting my hand over my mouth to shut off a scream, I died inside.

Should I take my chances on jumping out the second-story window into a snowdrift? Should I crawl under the bed to hide? My eyes took in every corner of the room searching for a safe escape, and I continued to implore the Lord to help me.

The lurching footsteps passed by my door without the knob so much as wiggling. I heard another door open, and then the steps continued up to the attic level of the house. There were sounds of something heavy being moved across the floor from one corner to another, then back again. Back and forth, back and forth. Who was it, and what was he trying to do?

Whenever the moving stopped, I could hear loud moaning and groaning. Was it from exertion—or pain?

Scared as I was, there was no point in my going back to bed. I'd never sleep with such carryings on above me. But where could I go at that hour of the night? I'd surely freeze to death if I tried to find an outdoor place to hide—

"A fine, brave, fearless missionary you've turned out to be," I berated myself. "Here you stand thinking about your own comfort and safety when upstairs there is somebody who needs help—desperately, from the sound of things. Why don't you get your clothes on and go up to see what you can do?"

Determining I would do what I could, fear or no fear, drunk or no drunk, I put the teakettle on. While the water was coming to a boil, I got dressed, my teeth chattering. I looked in vain for a flashlight, found a stub of candle, lit it, and made a pot of tea.

Moving the furniture just far enough that I could squeeze through the doorway, I gripped the candle in one hand, the teapot in the other, and stepped out. There was an open door a little distance down the hallway, and I could see stairs beyond it. The moaning and groaning were coming from that direction. My very heart shivering, I tiptoed to the stairway, the flickering light of the tiny candle making eerie shadows on the high-ceilinged, cobwebbed passageway. The bottom step creaked so loud it sent a further shiver through me. When I reached the second step, the moaning stopped. There was only heavy breathing, as if whoever it was had

71

settled down for the night. I stood and listened for a few minutes, persuaded myself that it wouldn't help if I disturbed somebody who had just gotten to sleep, and tiptoed back to my room.

I'd barely gotten inside when the moaning started again. Was it only my imagination, or did it sound worse than before? I headed for the stairway again, shook my way a little further up the protesting stairs this time before the moaning stopped again, then retreated shamefully back to my room as thankful as if I'd been reprieved from execution.

This happened four times. Each time before I'd set out, I'd pray, "Father, I'm sorry. I just can't do it. I just can't do it." Then He'd pour His vast ability into my vast inability, and out I'd go, still in fear and trembling, but knowing He was with me.

After the fourth trip, the moaning and groaning stopped for the night. With my door securely barricaded again, I took off my shoes and crawled into bed with my clothes on. By this time, my fright had spent itself, and I fell asleep. The next thing I knew, sunshine was streaming through the windows of my room. As soon as I was ready to leave for the mission, I inched the furniture away from the door and slipped out into the hallway. At the foot of the attic stairs, I listened, straining to pick up a sound of snoring or even breathing. There was only the dripping of a faucet and the scuttering of mice. Had the intruder left without my hearing him? Or had he died up there all by himself in his misery? I lacked the courage to find out. And to live alone in this strange place.

As soon as I got downstairs, there was a knock on the front door. Standing on the porch was a young Polish couple I remembered seeing in the mission choir. I invited them in, and they introduced themselves as Frank and Martha Zemmel. Tall and curly-haired, he was out of work hoping to find a job soon, and in the meantime, Martha earned such small wages cleaning house and baby-sitting that they could not afford to pay rent on an apartment. As they were explaining their plight to me in broken English, I had to exercise all my imagination to try to understand them. I saw that God had sent them as an answer to a prayer I hadn't even prayed yet. He was answering before I called, just as His Word said He would (Isaiah 65:24).

With more sign language and pointing than words, I let them know that I couldn't offer money, but they could live in the downstairs apartment if they would keep the snow shoveled from the sidewalks, the furnace burning, the ashes carried out, and the house clean.

Smiles of joy greeted my proposition and they assured me with a vigorous nodding of their heads that they could move in that very day. *Then* I told them about the goings-on of the night before.

Frank and Martha went up to the attic together, and I trailed along behind. The old hallway didn't seem half so scary in daylight. At the head of the creaking stairs, there was a big room with a rumpled bed shoved back in one corner under the eaves. Fresh scratches on the rough wood of the dusty floor marked the path over which the bed had been dragged back and forth, making all the racket the night before. But who was the mystery man?

"Mission caretaker live here one time," Frank said, "Mr. Perdick. He bad—fired—not come back. Maybe he sleep here last night." It was a logical explanation.

Our first order of business was to put new locks on all the outside doors so we wouldn't be in for a repeat performance.

"It's something I must do," I had told Mamma on our tearful parting the day I went to the mission. But from the beginning, I saw it was something I could *not* do. Never in a million years would *I* be able to accomplish anything for

73

the people of the mission community. Not even with the Zemmels coming to my rescue. But, if I was willing, God might choose to do the impossible Himself. All I could offer was my weakness, but I prayed that He would let me be the earthen vessel through which He would work. That prayer put me on the firing line . . .

9

"Tell Me, Pani . . . "

I WAS TO BE IN SOLE charge of the little Baptist mission set
in the midst of a community of steelworkers. Before my
coming, there had been three persons doing the job—a pastor and his wife, and a "pani"—an unmarried missionary
lady. Finances were bad, and they had all been let go. It
must have been out of sheer desperation the board had hired
a 25-year-old "pani" as inexperienced as I was for such a
position. Or perhaps they were trusting that the Lord would
provide helpers. He *had* already given me the Zemmels . . .

There were thirty-five different nationalities in the area,
speaking eighteen different languages, with only a scant one
percent of the population who understood two words of English. It was like being a missionary in a foreign country
after all.

How could I ever reach such people for God? At first, I
thought I would have to learn all the languages, and I started
in on it—Polish, Russian, Lithuanian—but I soon saw how
utterly impossible such a task would be. And since more of

75

the people seemed to speak Polish than any other language, I set myself to learning that one. The Zemmels were a real godsend to me. I had supper with them often in those early days, and while I helped them perfect their English, they helped me tackle the rudiments of unpronounceable Polish. I'd point to the bread and say, "Bread." They'd practice the new word until they got my nod of approval. Then they'd tell me their word for bread, *chleb,* and I'd practice that until their faces beamed at my accomplishment. Water was *woda,* a potato was a *kartofle,* soup was *zupa,* and the coffeepot was a *naczynie do kawy.* My "kitchen" vocabulary grew daily, but I was a long way from being able to carry on a real conversation.

In the meantime, God reminded me that there was a universal language that everyone already understood, His language of love. And as He gave me His love for the people, I began pouring it out, trying it first on the little children.

Every morning, I'd tromp the streets gathering up children to take them to the mission where they could be warm, have a bowl of soup, sing some songs, look at pictures. Some days there were thirty-five children in my little nursery school, twenty-three different nationalities. And God poured such a flood of His unfailing love through me, we hardly noticed that we didn't use the same language to express it.

It was amazing to see how quickly the children learned, once their little minds were unlocked from their fear of the strange-sounding foreigner in their midst. Soon they trusted me so completely that they became my interpreters. As I took each one home, I would smile at the mothers and exchange a few words through my pint-sized translators, inviting them to our women's group meetings on Thursday afternoons and to the church services on Sunday.

The mission itself, the place where I was expecting God to perform His miracles, was almost lost in the shadows of the huge structures across the street—an English Roman

Catholic church, a Polish Roman Catholic church, a Ukrainian Orthodox, and a Greek Orthodox church. Behind them all squatted an immense Communist hall.

The mission community was truly a melting pot of all nations. And how much melting was needed! Of prejudices, language barriers, fears, hopelessness—

For the most part, these New Canadians were a people with shipwrecked lives. Many of the men had come to the new world of opportunity, leaving their families behind, and they were discouraged at how long it was taking them to save up enough money to send to the "old country" so their wives and sweethearts could come to join them. Although most of them were, by nature, a religious people, they had no knowledge of a living Christ, of a Jesus who would live in their hearts and help them.

Making my calls to get acquainted with the members of my mission community put a real strain on the inborn shyness I always had with adult strangers.

One bitterly cold day, when the streetcars were not running, I walked nearly two miles to try to locate a certain small cottage set back from the street. Not really certain I had found the correct address, I was shivering more from apprehension than from the cold that day. When my almost frozen fingers tried to fumble through my notebook to recheck the house number, the wind threatened to rip the pages away. Going up onto the little wooden porch to make inquiry, I raised my hand to knock.

Before I could touch it, the door flew open, and a fierce-looking giant of a man grabbed my hand and pulled me inside. His great black moustache, bushy black hair, bristling brows, and eyes that pierced right through me made me think I had made a terrible mistake. While I stood quaking with fear, ready to scream and jerk my hand out of his grasp to make a run for it, he spoke with a terrible intensity, hurling at me the most significant question of my life:

"Tell me, pani, what new thing have ye learned about God?"

The fear drained out of me as I searched for an answer to the question spoken plainly but with a thick accent. My mind swirled with many things I had learned about God— that He loved me, that He died for me, that He could control my temper, that He could answer before I called, that He could keep our relationship from becoming ordinary, that He could communicate His love without words. . . .

But what *new* thing had I learned about Him?

I hesitated for another moment then burst out, "Well, I know that the Lord Jesus is here with me in Hamilton. He cares about me, He loves me here, just as He did in Toronto."

With that the man released my hand, threw back his massive head, and boomed with such joyous laughter that I felt suddenly completely at ease with him, secure in his presence. Why, here was a man who was *really* interested in the things of God.

Over a steaming cup of tea which chattered in its cheap white saucer as he handed it shakily to me, I learned more about him. His name was Mr. Lukasates (Loo-ka-say'-teez), and he and his wife had six children. She had a job scrubbing offices, but he was unable to work because his health was broken.

"Yah," he exclaimed, sitting down and running a giant hand through his thick black hair, "they told me I could never do it, walk almost all way from Siberia to Canada."

He sat quietly for a moment, his eyes lost in time. And then he brightened. "But I show them. I show them what Lukasates can do when he vants freedom." He told me how he had walked through Siberia grubbing for roots to stay alive, and then from Alaska right across Canada to the northern part of Ontario. Not only had he nearly starved to

78

death, but the bitter cold had frozen his lungs so he didn't dare venture outside the house in winter.

After that first encounter, I tried to visit Mr. Lukasates once a week, and never in my three years with the mission did I ever succeed in knocking on his door. No matter when I went, the door would fly open, just as it had the first time. And Mr. Lukasates' greeting was always the same, the burning question, "Tell me, pani, what new thing have ye learned about God?"

The necessity for having always a fresh blessing to share was a real turning point in my life. It taught me not to be a spiritual hitchhiker, riding contentedly along on something that happened years ago, but to expect God to be working continually in my life.

If He hadn't worked continually in those early days, I'd have been sunk. Miracles of grace were needed in every area of the mission work.

During the years when I had been experimenting with the promises of God, I had formed the habit of turning to Him when each naturally insurmountable need or problem came up. I'd search for a scripture that had a direct bearing on the situation and show it to the Lord.

"Lord, look. This is what Your Word says You'll do. Do you mean it? Does it work only for super-spiritual saints? Or is it for ordinary people like I am, people who are not so good, but who are depending on Your goodness and righteousness?"

One of my early experiments with proving His Word that He would supply all my needs (Philippians 4:19) took place while I was still going to school and working as a stenographer. In those days, when I got my pay envelope on Friday, I'd count out the money, putting certain amounts into each of my "budget envelopes." My tithe came first, then what I gave Mamma every week to help with household expenses, next an envelope for carfare, then another in which, by going without lunch, I was gradually accumulating enough for a new pair of shoes.

My old shoes were *so* worn. Every night, I'd polish the uppers to within an inch of their life, but the holes in the soles were getting bigger every day. I'd scrounge through the kitchen for new pieces of cardboard—a discarded cracker box, an empty oatmeal carton— Then I'd cut the cardboard to fit my shoes on the inside and make them wearable for one more day.

But on one particular Friday, I had finally saved enough for a new pair of shoes. It had taken a long time, because I had a very narrow foot, and bargain basements never carried shoes in the size that I wore.

I was putting the envelopes back in my purse, looking forward to the lunch hour when I could go to the department store and buy my shoes, when the Lord brought a name to my remembrance: Janice. Janice was a widow with two children, and I knew she had been having a difficult time financially.

"Give all your savings to Janice," the Lord seemed to be saying.

"But Lord! I can't do that. It's taken me forever to save up enough for a new pair of shoes. By the time I can save that much again, the old ones will have fallen apart completely!"

He didn't argue with me, but the thought hung in my mind so strongly that I couldn't think about my work: "Give all your savings to Janice. Give all your savings to Janice."

The harder I battled and tried to shove the thought out of my mind, the more insistent it became. At last, to get some peace, I rolled an envelope into my typewriter, clattered out the name and address of the young widow, wrapped the seventeen-fifty I had saved in a clean sheet of paper, and stuffed it in the envelope. Sealing the envelope and stamping it, I slapped it into my "Outgoing Mail" basket, muttering, "There now. I've done what I think You wanted me to do. But You'll have to do something about my shoes, Lord. They won't last another week."

That didn't sound much like a prayer, I realized, but it was the best I could do. At least I was being honest.

The next day, I was in the washroom when Miss Noble, the manager of our mailing department, walked in. Without any preliminaries she said, "Kay Golbeck, what size shoe do you wear?"

I blushed a million shades of purple all at once. My shoes must have looked worse than I thought, for someone to have noticed them. I was so embarrassed that when I opened my mouth to answer her question, no voice came.

"Here," she said, not waiting for an answer but standing on one foot while she tossed me a shoe, "try that on for size. Looks like it should be about right."

Hoping she wouldn't see my cornflake-box shoe-liner, I slipped my foot into her shoe. It was the softest leather imaginable, and it fit as if it had been made for me. Miss Noble looked relieved.

"I'm so thankful," she said. "I hate to have anything go to waste, and I'm going to be wearing special shoes on account of an orthopedic problem. The doctor says he doesn't know how long I'll have to wear them, but he sounded like it might be for a long time. If you don't mind wearing hand-me-downs, you'd really be doing me a favor and keeping the shoes from rotting on the shelf."

"He heard me! He heard me!" I was shouting inside. Outwardly, I managed a quiet, "Well, thank you. I'll be happy to wear your shoes."

Monday morning the mail boy, who made his deliveries roller-skating through the plant, dropped a big bundle on my desk. It was from Miss Noble. I took it behind a row of filing cabinets to open it—Not one, but three pairs of shoes scarcely worn at all! The heels were the height most comfortable for me—everything about them was perfect. God had supplied my need for a pair of new shoes above all I could ask or think.

As God continued to answer my prayers and prove His promises to me, my faith grew. So did my insistence on receiving the promises of God. That was to be of great value in my relationship with the women of the mission community. At first, I was terribly frightened of them, and I wasn't able to discover one who spoke a word of English—except Martha Zemmel, and she was working every day. My own "conversational Polish" was almost useless. There was simply nothing to work with.

Or was there something? There was a need. Could God use a need as a resource with which He could work in our midst? The idea began to stay in my mind as the days passed with no real breakthrough among the women. I didn't know what God's plan was, but surely He must have something in mind.

One of the things I had found out was that although it was a terribly cold winter, not one of the little children who came to our Sunday School or to the nursery classes during the week had any warm underclothing. I had plenty of warm clothing, and yet I stayed cold all the time. How utterly frozen the little children must have felt!

"Oh, what can I do for them, Father? Show me the way, Your way." One morning I learned that the Mercury Mills in Hamilton would sell mill ends of fabric very cheaply, and that afternoon I bundled up and made my way there through the blowing snow. When I had thawed out enough to speak, I explained who I was and what I needed for the children. Then I held out a dollar bill. In return, they gave me such a load of warm material, I had to let them summon a cab to take me back to the mission.

When I got to my room and dumped all that mountain of material on my bed, I realized that, working alone, it would take me until the next summer to stitch it up. Warm under-wear wouldn't help the children much if I didn't have it ready until July. I would simply have to get some help.

The next day, I went around to fifteen of the homes to which I had addresses. With the help of my Polish diction-ary, and many signs and gestures, I tried to get it across to the mothers that I wanted them to come to the mission that afternoon at two o'clock. Most of them came, women of all different nationalities, and sat down in the mission chairs. I wasn't intimidated by their blank looks, because I was full of excitement knowing that God had a plan, and I was to communicate it to them.

With lots of sign language, pointing to the material heaped on a table, I tried to pantomime for them a shivering little child, plucking pitifully at its too thin clothing. Then I made motions of using scissors, needles, and thread to turn the pile of knitted material into warm underwear. I mimed putting it on the shivering child, having the shivering stop, and a smile of cozy warmth take its place.

The women had started to beam when they sensed I was talking about their children. But had they understood? And did they realize I needed their help in making the garments?

My eyes scanned the blank-looking audience, and sud-denly a hand was raised. "Me? Help cut?" a timidly eager voice asked in broken English. I rejoiced at that, but when I questioned the woman to see if she had a sewing machine, I found that her English vocabulary and understanding were as sorely limited as my Polish.

Returning to my wordless communication, I tried, again by signs, to find out who in the group might have a sewing machine. I turned an imaginary wheel with one hand, guided some real cloth under an invisible needle with the other hand, and let my foot perform vigorous pumping action on a treadle that wasn't there.

The faces were still blank. They didn't see what I was get-ting at. Maybe the little Polish dictionary would have a word for sewing machine. Thumbing through, I stumblingly tried to pronounce it.

An explosion of unstifled laughter from two or three of the women spelled victory for me, and I laughed along with them. I must have pronounced the word in a ridiculous fashion, judging from how they held their sides and rocked with mirth, but at least I had made meaningful contact. One of the women came to my rescue then, pronouncing the word twice, very slowly, syllable by syllable. I repeated it several times until she nodded approval. But when I used the word as a question, looking at each woman in turn, they only shook their heads. Nobody had a sewing machine.

"Then we must pray for a sewing machine," I said. I folded my hands under my chin, closed my eyes, bowed my head, and said the Polish words for "Please, God, give us a sewing machine."

Then they thought I was really crazy, their expressions seeming to say, "Poor lady. Poor lady."

What I was suggesting was so preposterous to them that one woman bounced up from her chair across the room and opened her mouth to let forth a voluble stream of harsh-sounding words with machine-gun rapidity. I didn't have any idea what she was saying, but it sounded so fierce that if I could have disappeared through a knothole in the floor, I woud have done it gladly.

The other women gave the angry one their full attention, and when her tirade was finished, the timid little woman who had offered to help cut the material took sympathy on me. Haltingly, she barely whispered, "Zabrinski say 'No pray. *Buy* sewing 'chine.'"

I shook my head, pulled the linings from my pockets to show them I had no money, and repeated, "Please, God, give us a sewing machine," in Polish.

This time, there was no further burst of angry indignation at my stupidity, only cold silence. But my eyes had caught a glimmer of something—could it be faith?—in the face of the one who had come to my rescue with the whispered English words. I motioned for her to come up and stand beside me.

"Do you believe in Jesus?" I asked her.

"Yah," she said.

With the help of the dictionary and her own little knowledge of English, I asked if she would pray for a sewing machine in Polish while I prayed in English. I told her that the Lord who invented and understood all languages would hear us and grant our request. There were some snorts of disbelief from some who thought they understood what we were proposing to do, but all was quiet as the little woman prayed in Polish in front of the skeptics and then I prayed very simply in English.

That done, God gave me boldness to go to the calendar on the wall, circle the Tuesday a week from that day, and indicate by signs and the Polish word for sewing machine that I expected God to answer our prayers by that time. In the meantime, I enlisted several in addition to the timid volunteer to come on Friday so we could get all the little garments cut out for stitching up.

After the women had gone home, I was almost appalled by my audacity in asking God so openly for the miraculous provision of a sewing machine. What if He didn't come through? Then the women would *never* believe in my Lord. Although by now I had years of trusting Him to supply many needs in my own life, and I had always found Him faithful to do what He had promised, I had never made my requests known so openly in such an impossible situation. This time I was counting on Him to keep the promise of "Ask, and you shall receive . . ." (Matthew 7:7–8). We had asked, but—

It didn't help my confidence a bit that every morning for the next week the fierce-looking Mrs. Zabrinski came in to lord it over me, pouring out volumes of the incomprehensible consonant-laden syllables at me. I could only try to smile at her, supposing she was still scolding me for my foolishness in trusting God to supply something that only money could buy. When she had finished her spiel each day, angrier and angrier as the week went by, she slammed the door so hard the whole building trembled. I took her visits to mean, "Go and buy a sewing machine!" and if I had had the money, she'd probably have talked me into it. But the old stubbornness was still there, and I just kept petitioning my heavenly Father, doubling and redoubling the fervent urgency of my prayers with every passing day.

"Father," I implored Him, "I thought if they could just *see* a vivid example of how You answer prayer, they might soon ask You to come into their hearts and supply power to their lives." Just thinking about the wretchedness of much of the living I had seen throughout the mission community brought tears of real compassion.

"O, Father," I went on, "they're all having such a hard time. They need You so much. Won't You meet this need so they can see how wonderful You are and how much You love them?"

I awoke on Tuesday morning with an exhilarating sense of expectancy. This was the day. Either God would come through, or—I shuddered at the thought of what my daily visitor would have to say if He didn't. I wouldn't be able to wriggle out of it. The calendar was still hanging on the wall of the mission, the date boldly circled, the Polish word for sewing machine written large alongside it.

I dressed quickly, getting ready to leave the parsonage to do some errands before going to the mission a little later in the day. Just as I was about to go out the front door, the phone rang.

"Miss Golbeck?"

"Yes?"

"Will you be at the mission this morning?"

"I wasn't planning to be, but I can be, if there's any need."

"This is Jane MacDonald"—it was no one I'd ever heard of—"and yesterday my sister and I were walking along James Street, and in a store window we just happened to see a used, reconditioned—"

Every fiber of me strained to hear the impossible word. Would she say it? Was this God's answer to our prayers?

"Do you by chance have any need for a completely rebuilt sewing machine at the mission? If you do, we'd like to have it sent out to you this morning."

I fell to my knees rejoicing.

"I'll be there! Praise God! I'll be there!" I shouted. After that exuberance, I had to explain all the details of how God was using her to answer a very important prayer, and she rejoiced and praised God along with me.

When the men arrived with the sewing machine a little later, I had them set it up on a small wooden platform where no one could miss seeing it. Then I dragged our blackboard over beside the stage, and with the help of all the dictionaries in the mission, I wrote, in many languages, "Let us all thank God for sending the sewing machine."

When the women came in, their eyes nearly popped, and Mrs. Zabrinski who had been riding me so unmercifully was speechless for the first time in her life. I could hardly wait for bushy-browed Mr. Lukasates to ask me what new thing I had learned about God that week. My God could supply *all* our needs out of His riches in glory—even sewing machines.

It was the beginning of a new adventure in faith for most of the women.

I kept learning new things about God day by day. The people saw by how He answered their prayers that they had a loving heavenly Father who really cared for them. And I continually marveled at the big and little keys God gave me to open hearts to His love. There was some wonderful "new thing" about God to report to Mr. Lukasates every time I saw him.

87

10

Keys to Love

AMONG MY FLOCK, ALMOST every family had a boy or girl in a reform school for juvenile delinquents. Sometimes they were there because of misunderstandings arising out of language barriers; sometimes because economic circumstances were so hard they were almost forced to steal to stay alive; sometimes because of the rampant sin and lawlessness into which they found themselves thrust because of the hopelessness of every aspect of the dreadful depression years.

I heard of many families that were burning their furniture in an effort to keep out the piercing cold when they had no income to buy fuel. In some families, the children would have to take turns going to school, because there was only one pair of shoes to share among them. The awful poverty took its toll in many ways.

Not long after my arrival in Hamilton, I had made the discovery that desperate mothers were selling their teenage daughters for some man's weekend pleasure. These were middle-aged Polish men who had left their wives and families in Europe while they came to find work in the new world. Sometimes it took a very long time before they could save enough money for their families to join them. In the meantime, life was lonely, and such men were glad to pay the price of a ton of coal, or a warm winter coat in order to have the companionship of a pretty teenager for the weekend.

I was so appalled at my discovery that I wept. But I knew that tears wouldn't help. Action would. So I invited the girls whose characters were in jeopardy to spend the weekend in the safety of the parsonage. The Lord would keep twenty or so of them safe with me from Friday afternoon until it was time to return to school on Monday morning.

One mother, who spoke English, wore me out with her agonizing over her son. She'd be banging on my door with both fists every morning before eight o'clock. When I would let her in, she would be near hysteria, and the tale she had to tell me was always the same:

"My boy! He so terrible! He be hung on the gallows before he twenty!" She'd hardly come up for air before she'd repeat the whole thing again, getting louder with each recital. On and on she'd wail, like a perpetually broken record, until one morning I had had more than enough of it. I grabbed her by the shoulders and shook her, hard. Stomping my feet to insist on her full attention, I made her look into my eyes while I shouted at her:

"Stop it! Stop it! Stop it this minute, I say!"

I didn't loosen my grip until she had focused her attention on me.

"There's *nothing* wrong with your boy!" I told her. "There's not a thing wrong with Bill except that he's hungry, and he doesn't have enough to do. He's not terrible—but it's terrible for you to talk like that about him. What you must do is pray! Pray!"

I folded my hands under my chin and bowed my head to

show her what I was talking about. She might not be able to hear me over her loud lamentations which had started up again.

Feeding fourteen-year-old Bill and keeping him constructively occupied wasn't the easiest assignment the Lord had ever given me. Bill had an enormous appetite, and an insatiable urge for activity.

He and his cronies were all incurable truants, hanging around the mission when they were supposed to be at school, but they seemed always willing to do the little jobs that I parceled out to them.

There were many people tramping the streets in those days, in all kinds of weather, looking in vain for work to do. They'd always be cold and wet, so I'd keep a fire going in the basement room of the mission. There'd be a big pot of soup simmering on the back of the little stove, and freshly made coffee or tea. When I'd need to leave the mission to do my house-to-house visiting, I'd call Bill in.

"I'm leaving you in charge today," I'd tell him. "See that everybody gets warm, give them some soup and coffee if they want it, and show them the box of dry shoes and socks there beside the stove. Keep an eye on the cupboard for me, too. I know it's a big responsibility, Bill, but I'm trusting you to take care of it for me while I'm out." I'd remind him to see that the floor was kept mopped dry and clean from tracked-in snow so no one would slip and fall.

Time after time, Bill's youthful energies turned the simplest job into a highly complicated one. If I came back sooner than he expected me, I'd hear the wind-up phonograph blaring full blast while I was still halfway down the block. The floor would be sparkling clean, and one of the boys would be seated on the floor with all the polishing cloths under the seat of his pants. Bill would be holding onto his upraised feet, steering him around in time to the music—a rhythmic floor polisher in motion. Instead of scolding them for their nonsense, I'd have to join in their laughter.

Once I came in to find Bill swinging ape-style from the balcony to the chandelier in the middle of the room. Another day, he was sliding up and down the balcony railing, making it dazzlingly shiny. Bill never walked from one place to the next. It was one flying leap after another, and at the end of many days, I'd stop and thank the Lord for His miracle of keeping Bill and his pals from broken bones.

Keeping such boys out of mischief challenged all my ingenuity. So did filling the bottomless pits of their adolescent appetites. Once a week, I'd make a big pot of chili or beef stew—something filling and nourishing that didn't require a lot of meat but could be extended with beans and vegetables that were not quite so expensive. I'd bake a big chocolate cake for dessert, and invite the boys to have supper at the mission. When they had stuffed themselves with helping after helping of chili or stew and cake, I'd beam with satisfaction, thinking that for once they'd had all they could eat. But almost before the dishes could be cleared away, they'd be looking around again.

"Don't you have any fruit, Miss Golbeck? I thought I saw some apples on the table before supper."

I'd get out the fruit bowl, and they'd empty it before they went home to bed. From the way they acted, to have refused them the fruit would have resulted in their immediate death from starvation.

Years later, Bill came to visit me.

"What are you doing in Toronto, Bill?" I asked.

He hung his head.

"I can't tell you, Miss Golbeck, because I'm afraid you wouldn't approve."

"Not approve?" He really had my curiosity going. "What's the matter? Are you doing something you're ashamed of?"

"Well, no, not exactly."

"You're not stealing, are you?" I figured if I mentioned the worst thing that came to my mind, he'd go ahead and tell me what the trouble was.

"No, Miss Golbeck," he said, standing up a little straighter. "I'm not stealing—or doing anything else dishonest."

"You'd better tell me, then," I warned him, "or every time I pray for you, I'll be worrying myself to death about what kind of bad business you've got mixed up in."

"Well," he blurted, "I'm in a trapeze act in a circus."

"A trapeze act!" I just roared. "Well, you don't need to be ashamed of that. There are some wonderful people acting in the circus." We had a good time reminiscing about his capers with the mission chandeliers, the floor polishing, and all the rest of it.

After that visit, I was out of touch with Bill for a while, but years later, a six-page typed letter arrived from overseas where he was serving with the Canadian army.

"I know that you really prayed for me all those years," he wrote, "and because I saw God answering your prayers, I began to pray, too. One of the things I prayed was that I would meet a Christian girl, and that we could be married and have a Christian home together. Well, He answered that prayer, and gave me a wonderful wife, and four beautiful children. . . ."

The young man whose mother had been so worried that he would be hanged from the gallows before he was twenty had graduated from McGill University. After serving his country in the armed forces, he was given a very responsible position with the Bell Telephone Company in Quebec. He was in love with Jesus, he said, and served as an elder in his church.

I gave special thanks to God for letting me see how one of my charges had "turned out." I was learning to trust that

His love doesn't go forth and return void, but that it always accomplishes its purposes, in the fullness of time.

The Lord was constantly providing new keys to channel His love into someone's heart. And it seemed that the more difficult the "someone" was, the greater was the blessing that came when God broke through to him.

One day, when I was making my routine calls, I found myself in the neighborhood of a house where I had been calling every week for at least a year and a half. Always, the door would be opened fearfully, a scant two inches, and an unsmiling face would peer through the crack, but without returning my greeting. I would ask in Polish, "Please, may I come in?"

"No!" was the unvarying reply at that house, and the door would be slammed in my face. Each time, in a voice I hoped was loud enough for the occupant of the house to hear, I would say, "God bless you and your house," and I'd go on my way. On that particularly wintry day, I was eager to get my calling done so I could get back home, turn on the gas oven, and try to thaw out. But the Lord seemed to impress upon me an urgency that I was to make the call at the "unwelcoming" house as usual.

I tried to argue Him out of it: "But You know how it's been, Lord. She always slams the door on me. There's surely no point in my going there today. It's *so* cold—"

But the sense of urgency didn't go away, and I found my feet turning up the path leading to her front door. At my knock, the door was not opened, but a voice from inside called out a feeble "Come in," in Polish, of course. I could hardly believe she'd want me to come in, after all the previous rejections, but I opened the door and called out my usual greeting. I was met with another, "Come in," more feeble than the first one.

When my eyes got accustomed to the darkness, I could

see a woman lying on a couch. Walking closer, I saw that she was too sick to rise. She looked perfectly dreadful. In Polish I could have asked her, "How are you?" But that would have been a superfluous question. I knew how to say "God bless you" in Polish, too, but those words would have been empty unless I did something for her. Using the Polish dictionary I always carried with me, I asked her details of what I could do to help.

She let me wash her face and hands, fix her a cup of tea, straighten her bed, and do a few things to make her more comfortable. But the look on her face remained a hostile, unwelcoming one even while I was performing these little ministrations for her.

"Lord," I prayed under my breath, "there must be something I can do to reach this person for You." As I looked around the drab, unhappy room, I spotted a pair of boys' blue jeans with a wide hole in the seat of them. I picked up the pants and tried to let the woman know I'd fix them if she'd tell me where I could find some patching material. She raised a weak arm to point to a drawer in a cabinet. When I opened it, I found some squares of denim. In just a little while I had the seat of the pants sturdy enough for wearing again.

The sick woman never took her eyes off me during the whole operation. When I had finished, I folded the pants and laid them on the table. She gave me a weak smile that must have taken all her strength.

The next week, when I came to call, what a welcome I received! The woman was strong enough to meet me at the door, not opening it a suspicious tiny crack as she had for so long in the past, but flinging it—*and* her arms—wide to invite me in. Three short weeks later, the Lord gave me the high privilege of hearing her confess Jesus as her Savior.

As time went on, the woman began coming to our Monday night English classes. I learned that her husband was a

94

fine man who worked in the steel mills when work was available. They had five children, three girls and two boys, and every last member of the family became a staunch Christian before my work at the mission was finished.

Yes, I was learning that His love always works—in time. But sometimes situations arose in which I felt I had to see my prayers answered then and there—or else.

11

Bargaining with God

IT HAD ALWAYS BEEN very difficult for me to speak before a group. Even the reciting of a short poem would send me into agonies. In school, when I was called upon for an oral recitation, I would open my mouth, get a few words out, and then have to bolt for the washroom where I would be violently ill.

During the early days in Hamilton, the effort to hurdle the language barrier eclipsed any fears having to do with "public speaking." After a while, however, to my great horror, I learned that I was expected to speak to mission groups in churches in Hamilton and round about. When the invitations and requests began to come in, I made excuses, found someone else to go in my place, or wiggled out of it in some other way. But then came a day when I was supposed to take charge of a chapel service at McMaster University. All my usual escapes were blocked, and I was afraid I'd have to go and suffer through it somehow.

Well, I did just that, and my audience suffered with me.

I was so upset and nervous, I couldn't see a word on the piece of paper on which I had made my careful notes. The hour seemed to last forever, and when it was finally over, the infirmary nurse put me to bed. I had such a severe headache, that for three days I couldn't even lift my head.

Before I was well enough to go back to the mission, I was determined to have it out with the Lord. I never wanted to go through such agony again.

"Something's got to be done," I told Him. "Other invitations are bound to come, and there's simply no way for me to get out of all of them. You promised that You'd give believers victory over every circumstance of life, and here I am, living in the midst of utter defeat." I knew He could see my infirmary bed, the medicine on the bedside table, the ice-bag on my throbbing head. In those days, I was still at the bargaining stage in my relationship with God.

"Look, God," I proposed, "If You'll give me victory over this speaking business—if You'll show me that Your promise of victory is true in this situation—I will never turn down another invitation to speak for You."

With that, my head felt remarkably improved, and I rolled over and went to sleep. When I awoke, all trace of the headache was gone, and I was able to get dressed and return to the mission.

As I was unlocking the door, the telephone shrilled. A very agitated voice explained, "Oh, Miss Golbeck, "I'm *so* glad to reach you. I'm in the most awful predicament."

"I'm sorry. What seems to be the matter?"

"We're having an association meeting at our church tonight, and Dr. McLauren, who was to speak for us, has been taken ill—I hate to call anyone on such short notice, Miss Golbeck, but we're wondering if you can come to help us out, telling us about your work at the mission—"

"Oh, no!" I heard myself groaning inwardly as I sank into a chair and tried to swallow the sudden dryness in my mouth.

An association meeting was a big one—a meeting at which all the churches gathered for an extra-special service. Many people would be coming to hear the famed Dr. McLauren. He'd been a missionary to India and was one of the most remarkable speakers I'd ever heard. I *couldn't* take *his* place.

I opened my mouth to make excuses:

"I'm terribly sorry, I really am, but I've been away, and I've been ill, and—" but before I would get a word out, a Voice from deep within was asking me an embarrassing question:

"*What* did you promise Me, Kay Golbeck?"

"Just a moment," I said to my caller. "Can you hold the line, please?" I covered the receiver and turned my attention to that insistent inner Voice:

"*What* did you promise Me, Kay Golbeck? Didn't you say that if I'd give you the victory, you wouldn't turn down any request to speak for Me?"

"But, Lord! You didn't mean anything like this, I'm sure." I started to tell Him how famous and important Dr. Mc-Lauren was, and what an excellent speaker. When that didn't seem to budge Him, I indicated the towering stack of mail that had accumulated on my desk in my absence.

But the embarrassing question still hung in the air:

"*What* did you promise Me?"

I could see that I would have no peace until I went through with my end of the bargain. Uncovering the receiver, I said to the woman, "Yes, I'll come."

She was as profuse in her thanks as I was in my despair.

Was there *anything* I could say to the audience that would be at all interesting to them? There wasn't time to write a speech, much less to memorize one. I'd have to trust the Lord for the whole thing while I was on my feet—the content of my talk, knees that would hold me up, and all. It wasn't a comfortable feeling.

Before long, I was seated in the little cable car that would take me up the side of the hill to the church where the meeting was to be held. The wheels seemed to be grinding out a rhythmic "Will it work? Will it work? Will it work?" all the way to the top of the hill.

When I entered the church, far larger than I had remembered it, my heart plopped to my ankles. The place was packed! I was greeted in the narthex and ushered up to the very front row, feeling every eye in the auditorium studying the back of my head. I endured the preliminaries in an awful state of nerves, giving God occasional panicky reminders of His part of the bargain:

"Lord, You've *got* to do what You promised. You've got to!"

When it was my turn to go up on the platform, a dismaying thought hit me: I wouldn't *dare* let myself be sick, because I didn't know the location of the washroom!

My knees stopped shaking long enough to get me to the lectern. I gripped the sides of it and held on for dear life as I unfolded the little piece of paper with the few notes I had made. Then, for the first time in my life, I really looked at the audience I was to address. I blinked my eyes and looked at them again.

Why, they were only people!

I let my eyes go up and down the rows, from aisle to aisle. Still, only people! My relief was so immense, I just had to smile. And some of the people smiled back. All of a sudden, the butterflies that had been battling around inside me settled down for a siesta. I opened my mouth, said, "Let us pray," and asked God to let us all hear a word from Him that night. After the Amen, I delivered His message to His people.

What I said, I never knew, but when I was finished, I wasn't sick. I didn't have the slightest headache. In fact, I was so highly elated, I could have run down the mountainside instead of riding back in the little cable car. It had changed its tune from a scary questioning, "Will it work? Will it work?" to a singing affirmation, "It worked! It worked! It worked!"

After I got home, of course, the enemy had a grand time.

"That was all right for once," he agreed, "but what will you do if it happens again? With maybe an even bigger crowd? How do you know you will have the victory the next time?"

I was beginning to recognize the tactics of the enemy, and so I didn't dwell on the doubts he was trying to plant in me but tackled my mountain of mail instead.

The first letter was another speaking invitation. A church in an adjoining city wanted me to be their guest speaker for a thank-offering meeting in October.

"Not again," I groaned. "Not so soon."

Picking up my pen, I began to write a little note, expressing my polite regrets that circumstances prevented my taking time off to accept their gracious invitation. I went on to give several perfectly valid reasons why I found it impossible to be with them. As I lifted my pen from the paper, there it was again:

"What did you promise Me?"

I had to tear up the first note and write an acceptance instead.

The same thing happened as before. I went through untold miseries in advance of the meeting, and my heart plunged when I saw the size of the audience. But when I gripped the edge of the lectern and really looked at the individuals who made up the audience, God's love for them poured through me, a perfect love that cast out all fear. And the words that came from my mouth were received with gladness.

What I regarded as the biggest challenge of all came when I was asked to speak at a youth convention in Montreal. The other speakers were prominent men, very important in their fields. My inclusion on such a program, with such luminaries, seemed so ridiculous that I wrote and said I couldn't possibly come. But before I could sign my name to the letter and put it into an envelope, I found myself tearing it up and writing another:

"Lord willing, I'll be happy to come and speak."

Through the more than forty years since then, a number of persons have written to thank me for the help the Lord gave them in what He said through me at that convention.

There were other corners of my life where I needed special grace from God, extra help from the Lord. The areas of my own inadequacy varied from time to time, but always, as I tested His promise, I found it true: "Thanks be to God, who gives us the victory through our Lord Jesus Christ!" (I Corinthians 15:57, RSV).

Deliberately seeking new things about God grew to be a *daily* habit in the mission. If my spirits flagged, I was spurred on by the certainty that before the week was out, Mr. Lukasates would be asking, "Tell me, pani, what new thing have ye learned about God?"

I didn't know then that relying on God's promises to be true would be an actual matter of life and death to me before many more years had passed. In the meantime, however, I practiced being obedient to the things He told me to do. But seldom without argument.

One morning, I woke up early with a compelling urge to go and pay a call on a little Russian lady who lived nearly two miles from the mission.

"But Lord! Today is the day I have nursery school. Have You forgotten? I can't go to see the Russian lady this morning. I must be at the mission to teach the children. They'll be expecting me, and there isn't time to tell them not to come."

"No, you must leave everything. Get ready immediately and go to see her. She needs you."

It was a terribly blustery morning outside—a driving north wind, stinging sleet—

"Couldn't it wait until afternoon, Lord? After I take the children home? It'll be a little warmer then—"

"You must get ready to go right now."

"Well, all right, Lord. If You insist. But You'll have to send somebody to take over with the children. I can't desert them."

I began to dress for the cold walk, and I wasn't finished putting on the extra layers of clothing when a smiling young woman knocked on the door. A frigid blast practically blew her inside.

"Remember me, Miss Golbeck? I'm Polly Jackson, a student here at McMaster University."

I did remember her. She refreshed my memory about the details.

"When you spoke at the chapel a few weeks ago, I asked if I could help you at the mission some morning, and well, here I am." She flung her arms wide, laughed, and I invited her to sit down.

"What an answer to prayer you are," I told her, explaining my inner prompting to call on the Russian lady.

"I don't know why I'm to go just now," I admitted, "but I don't have to know the reason; I just have to be obedient to go. Perhaps God will show me why when I get there."

With the briefest possible instructions about the routine of the mission activities and the provisions for the little children, I thrust a handful of keys at her. She promised to stay with the children until I returned.

Walking as fast as I could, to keep from freezing to death, I reached the house of the little Russian lady in record time. Before I could get inside, she was down on the icy front stoop, hugging my legs.

"Pani, pani, I knew you come, I knew you come. They put me on street at noon if I not pay," she wailed. "All night I pray you come to help."

It was a true story I'd heard many times that winter.

Everyone was having a tough time keeping body and soul together. I encouraged the woman not to be afraid, but to believe that her heavenly Father would work out something.

"What are You going to work out, Father?" I asked Him. "What new thing are You going to teach me today?"

As I hurried to the bank to withdraw my small savings, the Lord gave me the names of two friends who might be able to make up the necessary sum. I was able to get in touch with them, get their contributions, and return to the little old lady by a few minutes before noon. I forgot all about the cold in my joy that I had been able to take part in His answer to prayer.

If I had been as obedient to the leading of the Holy Spirit in all other things, I might have been spared real catastrophe. But I was still headstrong, stubborn, too independent for my own good. And I didn't heed the warning protests of my physical body until it was far too late.

12

Doctor's Orders

DURING MY THIRD YEAR at the mission, I had completely accepted the principle that God would continue to present new challenges to me—and that He would enable me to meet them as I relied on Him. I had been afraid of things and people for so much of my life that I was deeply satisfied that I had acquired an inner sense of peace that had a no-matter-what label on it. It was truly a peace that by-passed understanding, because I sensed that something was coming up in my life that would be by far the hardest thing I had ever been called upon to face.

"Could it be a challenging change of work?" I wondered. I hardly thought that could be, because I knew I had not exhausted the challenge of the mission opportunity. I was only getting ready to *begin* some real work there. The first year had been spent in breaking down stone walls of fear, prejudice, bitterness, misunderstandings, pride, and racial barriers as well as national and language differences. The walls had crumbled as we laid the dynamite of prayer.

The second year had been spent in further preparation for my own understanding of the work and the best way to accomplish it. Now, in the third year, I knew I was in the center of God's will for me, and I thought I was about ready at last to do something for God.

Although I wondered about these things, there was no idle time to engage in prolonged speculation about them. I was merely curious. I'd always had a giant-sized package of curiosity. It had earned for me the title of "the walking question mark" during my school and career days.

"Am I going to be ill?" was another thought that whispered a time or two. I always promptly squashed that one. I couldn't possibly be ill—I couldn't afford to be. It was hard enough for me to manage while I was working—still sending a large portion of my paycheck home to my parents every month. It would be utterly impossible for me—or them—to get by if I stopped working.

Every day, insofar as it was humanly possible, I was walking His way, in the light of His leading. My joy in doing that was so great, I seemed to have wings on my feet, even when they were so tired they stumbled. We were walking together, He and I, whether it was four o'clock in the morning or two o'clock in the afternoon.

But I knew my health was not improving. Every day, in spite of my joy at all God was doing, I found it harder and harder to get going. And increasingly difficult to keep going once I got started. Sometimes I would start trembling for no reason at all.

One day while walking the children home after nursery school, I suddenly began shaking uncontrollably. Quickly I reached out to grab a lamppost to keep from falling down. It happened again the next day, only this time there was no lamppost or telephone pole within reach, so I tumbled down in the middle of the street.

"Your old horse is all broken down," I said as the children

105

gathered around in concern. "We've got to get her going, so you'll have to pull the old horse up and get her on her feet again."

Giggling, pushing, and shoving at each other, they scrambled to get hold of my arms. Then they counted "One-two-three, pull!" and hauled me to my feet again. This happened with increasing frequency, much to their delight, but not to mine. It got harder and harder for me to get up. I was often extremely dizzy. But the old stubbornness kept me from going to the doctor or acknowledging to anyone that I was really very sick.

I refused to admit even to myself what I knew from having pored over the pages of our family's medical book years before. I had all the symptoms of chorea—St. Vitus' dance. But I couldn't stop working. The people in the mission community—167 families, some with as many as thirteen children apiece—had become my family. They needed me. I would have to keep going. I took very seriously my place as a spiritual mother to my flock, and I thought I couldn't be spared.

We had a full schedule of activities. Monday and Friday evenings were set aside for English classes. That was a place where we expected the Lord to put us in touch with people who would become interested in His Kingdom. On Tuesday, we had a prayer service conducted in Polish by a Mr. Jersak from the Memorial Institute of Toronto. Wednesday evening was our Baptist Young People's Union meeting. Thursday afternoons, the women came for work meetings and devotional programs with hymns, scripture, and prayers in English and Polish. Friday afternoons were for the children's meeting, and another evening for the Boy Scout program. On Saturday, there were hikes, picnics, and other outside activities. Saturday evening was set aside for cottage prayer meetings in the homes of the parishioners. On Sundays, there was a morning worship service that combined the English and the Polish work so that parents who were lost in English-only services and young people who didn't care for Polish programs could attend the mixed services together. Sunday afternoon was the time for our Sunday School program, with the little children arriving half an hour early so they could learn a new song, hear a story told, or ask for prayer for some personal or family need. The Sunday afternoon Bible class for Polish adults was another project, and on Sunday night, there would be another service, all in Polish.

All this, added to the nursery school three days a week, and necessary parish calling, made for a full schedule, and I felt I was indispensable to it.

In June, I had to see a doctor after a bad fall. Strapping up my cracked ribs, he warned me about my damaged heart and suggested that I take it easy. I dismissed his warning with scarcely a thought. I knew that the rheumatic fever of my childhood had put a strain on my heart. But it had not limited my living in the past. I wasn't about to let it start running my life now. But I did know that I *was* very tired, almost too tired to do the things I thought essential. And I had so much pain that I seemed to carry a ton of weight even though I weighed barely a hundred pounds. People were always telling me I was much too thin, but I'd shrug and tell them I'd *always* been thin. Hadn't I spent six weeks on Grandma's farm one summer, eating all the time and drinking enormous quantities of rich milk every day, only to lose a pound and a half?

When I was still dreadfully weary after an unusually restful vacation, I asked the mission board for an extra month's holiday to strengthen me for the harder work of the winter months.

During my extended holiday, I decided to make some changes in a life insurance policy I had taken out for the benefit of my family. The thousand-dollar policy had been

issued to me—routinely, without a physical examination—
when I first went to work for Goodyear, but the change required a thorough physical examination. After looking me
over, Dr. Ferrier peered at me gravely before writing his
report. What he said was, "Kay Golbeck, unless you stop
work immediately for an indefinite period of time, you will
probably never be able to work again."

When I sputtered my protests, he agreed to let me try a
compromise for one month, under certain conditions. I
would have to take the special medications he prescribed,
limit my work to four hours a day, with bed rest in the afternoon, and submit to a whole host of other restrictions.

How they rankled! But I returned to Hamilton after my
prolonged holiday with a careful resolve to follow all Dr.
Ferrier's instructions and to live a life so close to God that
I would do only what He ordered. Sometimes I wondered if
I had been born with just two things—pain, and a great
compelling MUST that pushed me into the things that had
to be done, in spite of pain or physical difficulty. "A sixteen-cylinder motor in a four-cylinder chassis," was the
way Dr. Ferrier had described it.

But if I had found it difficult previously to meet the de-
mands of my job by working long hours, I couldn't begin to
accomplish enough in four hours a day. There were special
Thanksgiving programs to prepare, many classes to be met,
group activities and meetings to be conducted, the endless
round of hospital visiting, interpreting in outpatient clinics,
court sessions, interceding with welfare agencies, irate land-
lords, and a multitude of unclassifiable little extras that
cropped up daily, demanding immediate attention. Those
things couldn't be stopped, but I tried eliminating all but the
most essential home visitation, cancelling all outside speaking engagements, and every other appointment that was not
directly connected with the mission work.

My pain grew steadily worse, no matter how hard I tried

to ignore it. I reached the point where I was consciously leaning on the Lord not only day by day, but on an hour by hour basis, fervently praying He would send someone to help. When a Polish minister and his wife came just before Christmas, I wept with joy. There was no question about whether or not we would be compatible working together. I was overflowing with love for them and praise to God for bringing them to Hamilton. Carefully and prayerfully, we went over the work together. I told them all I had learned, introduced them to the people, and took them to the various agencies that could help them meet their needs in the community. I tried to hide from them the facts about my terrible physical condition, but they found out all about it before they had been at the mission for a week.

My secret came out one morning when I went to visit a sick woman who lived on the second floor of an apartment building. I was crawling on my hands and knees up the stairs to her room because I could no longer stand upright to climb stairs. Even climbing them on my hands and knees was extremely difficult, requiring such intensely concentrated effort that I must have failed to hear the front door open and close below me.

"Kay Golbeck! Good Lord! What's making you go up the stairs like that?" I recognized the booming voice of young Dr. Cornett. He had always been most kind to me and many of the mission community who could not afford to pay a doctor.

"Nothing's the matter with me," I lied, trying to brush it off. "I'm just a little tired today, that's all. So I was taking the lazy way up."

"The lazy way!" he snorted. "It doesn't look like a lazy way to me! You sit right where you are, young lady, until I come down from seeing Mrs. Merkowitz—that's where you were going?"

I nodded meekly.

"If I don't miss my guess, you're a whole lot sicker than she is. When I come down, I'm taking you right straight back to the parsonage. You'll stay put there until I can get a hospital bed lined up for you."

"But—" I began, only to run headlong into his, "No buts. That's an order."

"Yes, Doctor," I said. There didn't seem to be much point in arguing. Besides, I hadn't the strength for it.

"Well," I assured myself while I waited for him, "I guess I'll have to go to the hospital to let them see what they can do for me. But I'll be the best patient they ever had. I'll follow doctors' orders completely, and chances are, I'll be out within a week and ready to go back to work better than new."

I had never been more wrong in my life. And it was the mercy of God that I didn't know what lay ahead.

13

"You'll Never Walk Again"

I BEGGED THE YOUNG DOCTOR to let me stay out of the hospital until after the New Year, and he very reluctantly consented.

"But only on the condition that you'll spend your time resting, and not leave the mission house for anything," he warned, shaking his finger at me. I agreed, and almost the next thing I knew, it was January 2, 1936, and I was in Mount Hamilton Hospital with a very high fever. What had laid me so low, they said, was St. Vitus' dance, plus a particularly virulent attack of rheumatic fever with a heart that was playing all kinds of tricks. There wasn't an inch of me that didn't ache beyond belief.

But far harder for me than the almost unbearable pain was my indignation at having to submit to the ministrations of others for my most elemental needs. Someone had to feed me, bathe me, and take care of me as they would a tiny baby. How I rebelled against being so dependent on someone else! And the rebellion didn't go away until I became so

111

weak I'd have died without the help of others. Then, when I was too sick even to move, the indignation turned into thanksgiving.

More difficult than the pain and the loss of all independence was the heartbreaking sense of failure. Over and over, my inner being sobbed, "I've failed my Lord; I've failed the missionary board; I've failed the dear people He placed in my care; I've failed my family—" It went on and on, an unending dirge of accusation within me. I couldn't pray; I was too ill to read; there was nothing but reverberating self-condemnation: "If only I'd been careful to eat properly, to get enough sleep, to change my shoes and stockings when they were wet, to do only what *He* was requiring of me—" Anyone who'd already had rheumatic fever twice in her life should have known better than to live as I had been living.

I couldn't find any self-forgiveness inside me, and I wasn't able to receive His forgiveness either. It was such torment that my writhing spirit cried for help.

It wasn't a prayer, exactly, but oh, what an answer He gave. Our gracious heavenly Father brought to my mind, one by one, every verse of First Corinthians 13: " . . . Love is patient and kind. Love is not jealous or boastful. Love is . . . " and after every remembered verse, I heard Him say, "You gave My love. You gave My love to My children." By the time that comfort had continued through to the last verse, He had utterly removed from me the mountain of my failure.

It was true. He had literally poured His very own love through me, even in the form of a patch on a pair of lowly blue jeans, and that love could accomplish all He willed for it, no matter where *I* was. After all, there were *many* earthen vessels for His love, not just the one in which I dwelt. And so I began to praise Him for that.

I was going to need a clear channel, not one clogged with

112

self-condemnation, to receive from His hand what I would need for the blow that lay immediately ahead.

One day, six weeks after my admission to the hospital, I sensed that something must have been decided about my case, because everyone was suddenly very solicitous about me. Every nurse on the floor kept popping in to see if she could do something to make me more comfortable.

"Yes, I'm all right," I'd tell them. "No thank you, I don't need anything. Yes, they're taking good care of me."

I lost count of how many times the nurses dropped in or waved as they passed my open door. What was wrong with everybody all of a sudden? As far as I could see, it was just another pain-filled day. But everybody had a solemn vespers-for-one look, or one of forced gaiety that was even worse. Even the head nurse, known for a face that was as crisply starched and expressionless as her uniform, had tried to smile. And one little nurse had tears in her eyes every time she stopped in.

"Someone has bawled her out, given her a hard time," I told myself. But somehow I knew that her tears were for me.

Young Doctor Cornett was the one who came to break the news. How hard it was for him! He perched, tense as a bow-string, on the edge of a straight chair and looked at the floor. Before he opened his mouth, I could tell he had something to say that he didn't want to tell me. He talked about the weather, the political situation in Europe, hemmed and hawed, trying to be evasive.

"Come on, Doctor Cornett," I said finally. "No more stalling. No more beating around the bush. Out with it. What's the verdict?"

He cleared his throat, gently took my hand in his, and looked straight at me.

"Miss Golbeck, you know you've been checked and evaluated by the top medical experts. I hate to tell you, but after much deliberation and a careful review of all their findings, it is the undivided opinion of the experts that you will never—"

His voice broke, he swallowed, then blurted, "You will never walk again."

After a few minutes of dead silence, while that awful statement sank in to him and to me, he offered an explanation.

"As near as they can tell, your rheumatic fever settled in that hip you injured in a fall, and now there are at least three different kinds of crippling arthritis spreading into your spinal column. There's no way we know to stop it."

As I lay there speechless, he proceeded to give me what he must have regarded as a thin thread of hope:

"With your full cooperation, and the best care that medical science can give you, you *may* eventually recover to the point where you will be able to sit in a wheelchair under an apple tree—someday. Maybe you can write poetry, or do something like that . . . "

His voice trailed off lamely, and I found myself feeling more sorry for him than for me. To start with, I could no more believe the picture he was painting of **my** future than I could fly to the moon. I almost had to laugh, trying to visualize myself sitting in a wheelchair under an apple tree writing poetry—

"I don't believe it," I said firmly. "I can't believe it." All my old stubbornness was aroused as I went on telling him, "That may be what you doctors think. But you're just men. You can make mistakes. Surely this isn't the way my King wants me to serve Him. I *know* that God has another plan for my life. This will be just a short little intermission between acts," I insisted. "You'll see."

Doctor Cornett stood up, shaking his head.

"My dear Kay, I can't leave you with that false hope. You

114

will be far less frustrated if you will accept our verdict and learn how to make the best of it. In medical science, there's absolutely no hope for your recovery. But if you'll accept that, and not rebel against it, God can make your life rich even here."

He patted my hand and turned to go.

"I'll be back in to see you tomorrow," he said. "In the meantime, don't hesitate to ask the nurse for a needle. It's better to do that than to endure the pain for long periods of time without what relief we can give you."

When he had gone, the full import of what he was saying began to dawn on me. He was saying that I should not dare to hope. Not dare to hope to roam the woods again, to walk down a country lane— It couldn't be! I was only twenty-nine! I knew I was desperately ill, but I knew even more certainly that on the inside of me, the God of hope was not echoing the doctors' hopelessness. He was saying something else, loud and clear.

Later that day, I asked a nurse to read to me from the Psalms, and when she read, "But I will hope continually, and will yet praise thee more and more" (Psalm 71:14), I took it for a prophetic word, God's special promise to me. I would keep on hoping, no matter what. And I would praise Him more and more.

I wouldn't let myself wallow in the self-pity of defeat, asking why this calamity had happened to me. Instead, I'd look for victory, and my question would be, not "Why, God?" but "How, God? How are You going to get me out of this mess? The doctors say they can't do anything for me—what are *You* going to do to make me well? How are *You* going to heal me?"

I was to ask Him that question for more than eight years.

14

The Comforter

WHILE I WAITED TO LEARN *how* God was going to make me well, I tried to find out how to use this time of uselessness in such a way that it would glorify God. I didn't want to waste any of it in fretting about impossible alternatives that were not open to me.

I had endless hours for prayer for the sick patients all around me, for myself, for all who were dear to me in the outside world, for the dear people of my mission and the minister and his wife who had replaced me. I prayed for the staff members of the hospital, the nurses whose feet hurt, for the visitors who came, for the leaders of the government . . .

The necessity and desire to pray kept me in constant awareness of my heavenly Father. We had an inter-com system, always open for thoughts as well as spoken words to flow between us. All along, I realized that I must win a victory over that inner anxiousness that said, "I must hurry and get well. I can't stay here any longer. I must get well. I must, I must, I must!"

I knew that as long as there was fear and tension in me, I could not improve. And so I learned to ask Him to let me rest in His rest, partake of His peace. He heard and answered, again and again, from the pages of His Word. One day He illuminated two verses of the eighteenth psalm for me: "O Thou God, Thou wilt light my lamp. My God, Thou wilt make my darkness shine . . . By God's help, I can leap a wall." I took them as His promise to me that He would make me able to go walking and leaping again, someday. In the meantime, He would "make my darkness shine." That meant He would have to make me able to overcome pain, boredom, anxiety . . .

I began to experience Him as my Comforter. There was His continual inner assurance that I would have to bear nothing alone, that He would always be in me to help, bearing the heaviest part Himself. Gradually, I could feel His presence taking the place of the aching emptiness I felt for the mission folk who had become my family. Instead of loneliness for them, I found myself satisfied with His dynamic and gripping presence. It was more than enough—sometimes.

One particularly poignant reminder of God's all-sufficiency came in the form of a brown paper parcel a mission Sunday School teacher brought me one day when she came to visit.

"Mr. Lukasates sent this to you," she said. "His children are in my class, you know."

I slid the string from the bulky bundle, and found a white tissue wrapping beneath the brown paper. Loosening it, I caught my breath. Inside was a beautiful soft leather pocketbook, intricately laced together, with a richly detailed design on the front and back—all trees and flowers that I loved so much.

"Mr. Lukasates made it for you, Kay, in the crafts class at the TB Sanitorium," my visitor said. "He was taken to the TB hospital just before you were brought here, you know," she reminded me.

I nodded, too full to speak for a moment, just thinking of all the loving hours Mr. Lukasates had spent pouring his limited energy into that purse for me. I could see that it was made to last a long lifetime, a real token of his faith that I would recover.

"Is he getting any better?" I asked my friend when I could trust my voice not to break.

"Well, I can't say that *his* health seems much improved," she said, "but from the first time I went to visit him until now, there's been a tremendous change in the ward around him. It was such a gloomy place to start with—but now it seems the whole place is brighter, somehow. Maybe it's just that I'm getting used to it, but somehow I believe that God is really working there. And do you know what Mr. Lukasates asked me the first time I went to see him—and what he's asked me every time since?"

"Praise God!" I exclaimed. "I know that Mr. Lukasates is all right if he can still ask his favorite question." Then I told her about his burning intensity the first time he had asked *me*, "Tell me, pani, what new thing have ye learned about God?" I told her, too, what some of my answers had been, and my faith was given a real shot in the arm that day. My visitor and I decided that Mr. Lukasates must have been asking the same question of his fellow patients, and that wherever that question was asked—and really heard— things were bound to get better.

It was good to have the pocketbook as a reminder that I could be continually learning new things about God in the hospital.

Soon after the pocketbook arrived, I was moved to Oakville Hospital, about halfway between Hamilton and Toronto, and Mr. Lukasates and I lost track of each other. I never heard from him again. But hardly a day passed when I didn't remember to ask myself his wonderful question—and to hear God's wonderful answers.

But not all days were days of victory even then. Sometimes I spent hours rebuking myself for too little faith, for having more than a ghost of a wish to give up, for flinching at the thought of bearing more days of pain. But for the most part, I believed there would be victory, that I was only being prepared for the next step and when I was ready, God would make it known to me.

I didn't know I would have to die first.

To keep me from perishing with the boredom of the unending sameness of daily routines, the Lord showed me much that I could do with my mind to escape the four-wall limitations of a hospital room. Early in my illness, I had asked a friend to bring me a little red notebook from the ten cent store—"Red is for courage," I told her—in which I made lists of all the things I would do and all the places I would go when God made me well enough to be a doer once more. I planned my itineraries carefully, figuring distances on maps in my head, making mental lists of the special clothing I'd need to put in my suitcase for different climates. When I tired of touristy imaginings, I'd be an architect, visualizing the floor plans in different places I'd lived, figuring how they could have been remodeled for greater efficiency or comfort. Working out an improved traffic pattern for the old mission house was a special challenge, and mentally rearranging the contents of its cupboards kept my thinking workshop busy.

I spent a lot of time in Bible study, and in reading good books I'd never gotten around to in the past. Hours of intercession for other patients made the nights fly swiftly by. The nursing Sisters would tell me which patients were scheduled for surgery the next day, and I'd eagerly anticipate a good report when the surgeons were finished with their work. When there was interminable waiting for a drink of water or someone to lift a sheet from painfully swollen feet, He taught me not to fret at the delay but to marvel at His gift of patience to endure.

Routines were sometimes varied when I'd be ambulanced to another clinic or hospital so that some new treatment could be tried. From Mount Hamilton Hospital, I was moved to Oakville, then to St. Joseph's in Toronto, down to St. Michael's, back to St. Joseph's. I was a guinea pig for every new thing—a cup of sterile milk injected into my hip every day, the gold cure . . . While I prayed over each new treatment, expecting God to use it to heal me, nothing worked. Large doses of this and that seemed only to accelerate the downhill plunge recorded on all my charts.

During all this time, friends provided all my material needs, giving me more nightgowns and bedjackets than I could ever wear out, more dusting powder and cologne than I could ever use up. They also inspired me with their courage and let me feel the warmth of their love, the strength of their prayers. They were always cheerful, expectant, trusting, believing I was learning the things God wanted me to learn in this stage of life. Every time I was extra weary, every time I had spent a night in discouragement, weeping at the pain, every time I was on the verge of giving up, someone would send a little bit of encouragement in the form of a letter, a card, or a note, usually quoting some scripture God had given them for me.

One day when I had done a lot of inward complaining about my lot, I received a letter from my friend Major Walter Steven of the Army Chaplain Service. We had gotten acquainted during the mission years when I served with him on the Interdenominational Board of Religious Education. How guilty I felt when I read,

I was glad to hear that you are still finding opportunities to bring strength and comfort to others even during your weakness. Keep the flag flying always, Kay. I know you have already discovered that God can use any situation which is honestly surrendered to Him.

His unearned praise made me so ashamed. "O Lord," I prayed, "forgive me all my inner grumbling, and make me like I ought to be on the inside as well as on the outside. Help me to *know* that You're working all this for good in Your plan for my life."

Buoyed by the faithfulness of my friends, blessed by their prayers and by His answers to mine, I wrote in my journal,

God gives the courage to face these black days and blacker nights. He helps me to witness to the joy within. Sometimes I want to tell everybody how terribly my body hurts, how utterly and completely weary I am, how numb I feel emotionally, how muddled my head seems to be. But the Father knows. No one else should be burdened with my grumbles. They all have enough troubles of their own, so it's better just to laugh along. . . . Friends, loved ones, family, work, hopes, and dreams all seem so far away. There seems to be a heavy curtain between them and me, making all these things unreal. Only Christ is real. The awareness of His presence is more vivid and sweeter day by day. How I long to show Him the depth of my love.

I spent many hours conjecturing what the future might hold, pondering all sorts of schemes. Then I would chide myself for such a waste of time, remembering that God already had the plan, and I needn't give it a thought. I had only to be submitted to His will, and He would work it out.

"This is only a brief interlude," I told myself on a relatively "good" day—"one of the 'rests' to round out the symphony of life."

On a particularly "bad" day, I heard from the chancellor

of McMaster University where I had attended some night school classes while working with the mission:

> I think you have been marvelously brave about this whole thing. I would have given weakly in and railed at the universe and been in bad humor generally. But you have been so plucky and sweet through it all. I can't say how much I admire you for it.

No earthly person knew how *un*brave I had been, how *un*sweet inside, how *un*worthy of any admiration my inner attitude had been. But God, looking on my heart, showed me my true self, led me to repentance again, and kept working to rid me of the self that did not truly glorify Him.

During the years, our Lord proved to me over and over again what a Comforter He is. One night I was wakened at three minutes after midnight by a strange light in the room. One of my earthly father's favorite hymns was vibrant on the air: "When they ring those golden bells for you and me . . . " I knew that his bright blue eyes were closed and that he was passing from this life into the next one. I thought about his hands warming my knees, and about the sled rides and the walks we used to take . . . But my sorrow that I would never see him again on this earth was overwhelmed by God's comforting assurance that we would be together forever in the eternity of heaven.

It was nearly ten days after I had sensed his passing before I saw any member of my family. As my sister Edith came into the room, she burst into tears.

"Don't worry, Edith," I told her. "I know that Father's gone on."

"How did you know?" she cried. "We told the nurses not to tell you until one of us could come to be with you."

"The nurses didn't tell me," I explained, "God did." Then

I described to her the ethereal light and the heavenly music.

"What time was it, do you remember?" she asked.

"Three minutes past midnight."

"That was the time he died—exactly," she said, sinking into a chair. Then I was able to share with her the comfort by which the heavenly Father had comforted me. Together, we were so caught up in His presence, she had to be reminded when visiting hours were over.

During the time when He was comforting me in the death of my father, God was also filling me with a kind of deep, quiet, unutterable joy about my own situation, even though the walls of the chronic medical ward seemed to exude despair and suffering. With patients about me filled with pain, and the dread of more pain, I was blessed to lie cocooned in His grace, as if He were bearing the pain in my body for me. His peace fell like a gentle spring rain that eased over my body and my spirit as a mother eases a blanket over her sleeping child. It was as if I had an existence in the midst of pain, but another one outside and apart from pain, with a continual river of joy flowing under it all.

While I marveled at all this, I came to a valley, darker and deeper than I had dreamed possible. After six years in the hospital, I suddenly became critically ill—in such constant awful pain from the least vibration of things around me that I was moved from the busy ward to Room 27, the solitary "dying room." Oh, there was no label on the door, and the hospital personnel didn't call it the "dying room," but everyone knew that's what it was. The nurse who wheeled me down there was terribly ill at ease.

"I hate to put you in this dull room all by yourself, Miss Golbeck," she apologized. "But the Mother Superior thought you'd be more comfortable here. It's so much quieter than that noisy ward—and you won't hurt so often from the building shaking itself down everytime someone crosses the floor."

"There's no sense in beating around the bush," I said. "I know what the room is for, and I know why I'm being moved there. But I'm not going to die; I'm going to get well. God's going to heal me; you'll see." She didn't argue, just blushed furiously, and I wished I felt as confident as I sounded. The room brought back a flood of vivid, painful memories—of baby Harvey, and the assurance I'd had that he would be healed. But Harvey had died.

As I was wheeled into the same dying room with the same cracked plaster and paint, I had assurance that I, too, would be healed. But was that a false assurance, too? Was I only fooling myself? Was my short trip down the hall into the dying room the last trip I would ever make anywhere on this earth? Was my little red notebook only a joke?

"Lord, are You really going to heal me? When, Lord? How, Lord?"

For days, it didn't seem to matter. Nothing did—not even the fact that every worldly thing I held dear—friends, books, music, letters—all were taken from me. Only medical staff popped in fleetingly to do what had to be done. The pain was all-consuming, lessened only slightly by countless drug injections. I thought only of being rid of it. And I hung onto a thin thread of sanity only by continual prayer.

God wanted to teach me how to appropriate His promises for the needs of every moment. Many days, my heart cried out, "O God, You promised to help me! Please help me now! Help me not to scream when the nurse turns me over. Help me to bear this awful pain! Help me not to become a drug addict with all this medication. O God, help me! Help me!"

One day as I continued to cry frantically, my teeth clenched, my knuckles showing white as I grabbed the frame of the bed, a still, small voice seemed to whisper reassuringly, "Yes, I *did* promise to help you, My child. So why don't you act as if I *am* helping you right now?"

Hearing that, I saw that I wasn't to claim His promise for

124

some future help, but that I was to take hold of His help by faith in the immediate *now*. But how? How could I do this? The key was to thank Him for a gift He had already given me.

"Oh, thank You, Lord, thank You that You *are* helping me now, this very moment."

He was calling me to a new level of faith, faith that could do far more than ask for the promises of God, faith that could actually *receive* them as a present reality, right now; faith that could *be* the substance of things hoped for, the evidence of things not seen. This new kind of faith became a refrain on my lips:

"God is helping me right now. Right now, God is helping me."

As I began thanking Him for giving me the help I needed, I found that thanksgiving brings release. As my body began to relax and I trusted Him to fulfill His promise in my body, the pain was not quite so unbearable. And strangely, the more I suffered and the weaker I grew, the surer I became that my case would *not* end as my brother's had, but that God would make me every whit whole—this side of heaven.

But first, there was another lesson to be learned, another promise to be proved:

"Lo, I am with you always" (Matthew 28:20, RSV); "I will never leave you, nor forsake you" (Hebrews 13:5, RSV).

He *was* with me, so palpably and preciously that I needed no one else. For two years, His promise that He would never leave me nor forsake me was demonstrated continually. The room was so filled with His presence I was glad *not* to have visitors, for fear their presence might spoil the wonder of what He and I shared together. It was impossible for me to be lonely.

And then came the day when I experienced for myself the truth of the Twenty-Third Psalm:

"Yea, though I walk through the valley of the shadow of death, I will fear no evil, for thou art with me."

According to the hospital records, I walked through that valley on November 20, 1943. And for me, the valley of the shadow became a glorious heavenly garden, filled with the presence of my Lord who would never leave me, in life or in death. There was no evil to fear, only His instruction to be obeyed:

"Go back. I have work for you to do."

15

"The Prayer of Faith
Shall Save the Sick . . . "

WELL, I HAD COME BACK, all right. For more than four
months after my return from heavenly places, I had been lying immobile, pain-filled, waiting. Waiting. Hoping. Seeking. Trusting.

My mind flew back again to that long-ago day when I
rode the little cable car to the church where I was to speak
before a group. The wheels had sung out a fearful rhythm,
"Will it work? Will it work? Will it work?"

The answer that day had been a joyful affirmative, "It
worked! It worked! It worked!"

But what would be His answer to me today? Would
anointing with oil and the prayer of faith "work" for me?
Was I about to learn a wonderful new thing about God? Or
was I— No, I wouldn't let myself think about the alternative.
I couldn't bear the thought of one more day of pain.

"Lord, *are* You going to heal me?" For years, He had
seemed to be saying yes in spite of the steadily deteriorating
condition of my body. And now that He had told me there

was work for me to do, I was more certain than ever that His answer just had to be yes. My body couldn't last much longer. It had passed its limit of endurance.

"Lord, *when* are You going to heal me?" Every cell within me seemed to question, "Now, Lord? Please, Lord, can it be now? Today, Lord?"

"Lord, *how* will You get me out of this mess?"

He alone knew the answers.

On May 6, 1944, at 8:00 P.M., while it was misting rain outside in the Canadian springtime, there was a brief ceremony in the dying room. I didn't want anything emotional, and it wasn't. Two elders, a Mr. Reeder and a Mr. Swayze, were there, along with the Reverend Joseph McDermott. Together, we simply believed God's Word, and claimed His promises. All three men prayed earnestly and fervently and tearfully for the perfection of health in my body. Mr. Mc-Dermott opened a small bottle of oil, over which he had already prayed a prayer of consecration, and dipped his finger in it.

"According to Your direction, Lord, we claim Your promise of healing." With his forefinger, he touched my fore-head and the base of my throat, making the sign of the cross. The two elders stood on either side of the bed, each holding one of my hands. Mr. McDermott rebuked the disease in the name of Jesus, and closed his prayer by saying, "We await the carrying out of the healing grace of our Lord to every cell of this body."

No one gave the command for me to do the impossible. No one told me to get up and walk. But instead of being surprised or disappointed at that, I found myself overpowered with sleep. I don't even remember the men leaving the room, I was so drowsy.

My out-of-the-ordinary sleepiness caused an awful stir. In those days the nurse would come in and take the spread off the bed and fix you up for the night. They always had a

few extra things to do for me. There were three pillows to
adjust so my bones wouldn't poke through my skin, something to put under my feet to lift my toes off the bed to make
me as comfortable as possible, and a routine check on the
two 500-watt bulbs that burned over me day and night.
When a nurse came in to do these things, I mumbled,
"Please, just let me alone tonight. Don't bother me about
anything."

I was *so* groggy, but through the fog I heard a protesting,
"Oh, but when the supervisor comes around to check behind
me, I'll get in trouble."

"I'll tell her it was my fault," I murmured. "Please go, and
let me sleep."

Well, that got the supervisor on the premises in a hurry.
And she was so concerned about my unusual sleepiness that
she called the house doctor to check me over. But they all
settled down after a little, and the next thing I knew, it was
six o'clock in the morning, and Claudine was there, waking
me up for my morning medicine.

"Wow!" she said. "What a sleep you've had, Kay! I've
been in twice to give you a needle, but Sister said I was not
to wake you. She stayed with you most of the night. How are
you feeling this morning?"

"You mean it's morning already?"

Through the fogginess of my sleep-dulled mind, I remembered, "He giveth his beloved sleep" (Psalm 127:2), and
chalked up another scripture promise proven in my life.

Then, suddenly, I was wide awake, electrified with a star-
tling revelation:

"Why, I haven't any pain!" I exclaimed to Claudine. "For
the first time in my whole life, I don't hurt anywhere! I don't
need any medicine! But please let me have a drink of cold
water. My mouth is so dry—"

Surely God must have given me a heavenly anesthetic. I
had just had my first full night's sleep in fifteen years! My

heart was nearly bouncing out of me. Dare I try to move?

While Claudine dashed off for my glass of water, I prayed, "Oh, Jesus! Thank You, thank You, thank You! And please don't let me make any mistake. Show me each step, so I won't lag behind You and I won't run ahead of You. Tell me plainly what I'm to do to take hold of the perfect healing You've bought for me.

"What am I to do first?"

The instruction came with such distinctness there was no mistaking my orders:

"Take your own drink of water."

Simple enough? Not when you've been face down in a frame with shoulders, elbows, hands, fingers, and jaws locked in place for over two years. What He was asking me to do was humanly impossible. But I had learned that sometimes such an act of faith is part of what's required if we're to receive all that our Lord wants to give us.

When Claudine returned with my glass of water, she did what she had been doing for years: she stuck a glass tube in the water and moved it toward my mouth.

"Not today, Claudine," I told her. "Today, I'm supposed to take my own drink of water." The look on her face told me that she was believing too!

"How far do you think my arm would reach?" I asked her.

She knelt alongside my bed, measured with her arm, and then held the glass an arm's length from me. It seemed as far away as the moon, but even in the midst of that realization, my heart was singing out that all things are possible with God. With every fiber of my being straining toward the goal, I willed to move my arm. The bed was sopping wet with my exertion.

And as I tried, the impossible happened. My shoulder unlocked, then the elbow. I watched in fascination as the arm reached out, the hand and fingers opened to grasp the glass and bring it to my mouth. As I held it to my lips, my jaws unlocked, and I drank the whole glassful without stopping.

Every pain had disappeared. Every joint was suddenly set free. Such joy filled me, such praising of God welled up inside me, that I felt my spirit turning cartwheels, and I almost thought my body could do it, too.

Claudine was stammering with joy.

"K-K-Kay, I'll—I'll bring you anything you want f-f-for b-b-breakfast." Both of us knew that in spite of the fact that I'd had nothing for months except liquids, now my digestive system would be able to handle anything.

"Oh," I said, "I'd like something to chew—the crunchiest, hardest piece of toast you can make. And a poached egg. And a whole pot of coffee."

She bent to embrace me before she left to get my breakfast. Both of us were about to burst with happiness.

While Claudine was gone, I was busy praying.

"Father, would it be all right with You if I turned over? I want to turn over so badly—but I don't want to be out of Your will in anything. You're going to have to guide me every second of this day."

Words that sounded like scripture flashed through my mind, giving me complete confidence and assurance: "As thou goeth step by step, thy way shall be opened up before you." And as I waited, rejoicing, the instructions came, just as clearly as if He had been standing beside me in the flesh, speaking with a human voice:

"Yes, you may turn over. And you may ask for one pillow."

When Claudine walked in with my breakfast on a tray, she nearly had a conniption. I was lying on my back. For years, I had begged to be turned over, but the doctors always forbade it.

"I may even have a pillow," I told her when she had recovered enough to hear.

Both of us were above doctors' orders that day, and she

brought the pillow and tucked it under my head, wondering if my back would snap and break in two. But it didn't, and oh, how good it was to look up at the ceiling instead of down at the floor.

Next, Claudine put my tray before me, and I fed myself. Just being able to chew the toast was like being in heaven. And the poached egg far surpassed any gourmet's dream.

When the shift changed for the nurses, word spread of my miracle, and every nurse I'd ever had came running in to see me. When someone came in to make my bed, I announced, "I'm going to sit up in the chair while you make the bed. It's high time my mattress was turned over."

Well, the startled nurse didn't put me in the chair, she went running for her supervisor, who bustled in at a trot.

"What's this nonsense, Kay, about your thinking you can sit up? Preposterous!" It was plain she didn't believe my miracle.

"Yes, Sister," I said, laughing out loud. "I'm going to sit up in a chair while they make my bed this morning. Will you hand me my robe, please?"

The next thing I knew, the Mother Superior was in the room, trying to reason with me.

"Kay Golbeck, this turning over without permission is bad enough. But surely you have sense enough to know that we simply can't let you sit up in a chair—unless we have the doctor's permission."

"Yes, I know, Sister," I laughed. "We can't even *sneeze* without the doctor's permission." But then I got serious and explained why I had to sit up.

"Last night some friends came and anointed me with oil and prayed for a complete miracle in my body. You can see that at least some of the miracle has happened. But how will I know if God has given me a total miracle if I don't do as I'm told? He's the One who gave me permission to turn over, and to have my head propped up on a pillow. And you can see, that worked out all right. He's given me permission to sit up, too."

"Well, but we're supposed to have all our orders in writing," she said lamely. "Otherwise we'll get in trouble."

"Well, that's no problem either," I assured her. "Just bring me a pencil and a piece of paper, and I'll write the order and sign it myself."

She flounced out of the room, muttering something about going against the will of God, but soon returned with a typed-out order which she presented to me for my signature.

"Kay Golbeck," I wrote. The signature was kind of shaky, not surprisingly, since I hadn't held a pen for years, but the Sister accepted the piece of paper, folded it and stuck it in her pocket. Then she helped the other nurse lift me into the chair.

Wonder of wonders! My back didn't break, my knees bent where they were supposed to, and my feet rested lightly on the floor. Still no pain!

Listening for my inner instructions, I told the nurses, "You won't need to put the heat cradle back over my bed. I won't be using that any more." By that time, their utter amazement had overcome their arguments, and they didn't protest, just carried it away.

"What next, Lord?" I asked Him while they were out of the room.

Again the instruction came, unmistakably clear:

"You may take four steps—with help." I put on my stockings and slid my misshapen feet into shoes that had been empty for eight and a half years.

When it came time to get me back in bed, one nurse took my right arm, another my left. They helped me to a standing position, and I put my full weight on my feet. Excruciating pain shot through my feet and ankles and radiated up my shrunken legs.

"Oh my feet! I forgot my feet!" I cried out. They had been

133

turned for so long, lying flat, that I could hardly bear the
pain of my weight on them. But I was determined, pain or no
pain, to take the four steps He had permitted me, just to see
what would happen to my legs. On the first step, my right
knee buckled. On the second step, the left one gave way. On
the third step, both wobbled a bit, but the fourth step was
accomplished with both knees behaving exactly as knees
ought to. And they never buckled again.

From the bright blue sky that peeked through the high
windows of the dying room, I could tell the sun was shining.

Fifteen doctors came to see me the next morning.

The chief of staff had me sit on the side of the bed, and
he poked and probed as he explained to his colleagues,
"Gentlemen, just last week, the mere vibration from someone walking across the floor would cause such unbearable
pain in this patient that we had to give her morphine."

The doctors shook their heads in wonder and disbelief.
The chief went on to use a lot of technical terms, explaining
that all parts of my anatomy had been locked up.

"Now, suddenly, for some inexplicable reason," he went
on, "she has no pain, and it's obvious that all the joints are
free."

"Simply unbelievable. Unbelievable," I heard one of the
doctors mutter. Every eye was fixed on me as if by staring
they could find the cause of my remarkable recovery.

"Are you *sure* that doesn't hurt?" the chief doctor asked
me again as he flexed my arms and neck, lifted my legs, and
tapped up and down my spine.

"Not a bit," I assured him. "Not a bit."

When the doctors left my room, Claudine came bursting in.

"That old atheist!" she shouted. "He makes me so mad.
He can't believe a miracle when he sees one. Why, I bet he
wouldn't even believe if a miracle happened to *him!*"

"Wait a minute," I said, trying to slow her down. "Just

think how long it has taken you—and me—really to believe
that a thing like this could happen. And both of us knew
we had God's word for it. That poor doctor just has *our*
word. We can't blame him, really. After all, it's only by
God's grace that we ourselves believe, isn't it?"

"Well, I guess so," she said, tugging her skirt down.
"You're probably right about that. Guess we'll just have to
pray harder for him, huh? That something will happen to
make him realize God is real and that He hasn't stopped
working."

I could agree with her about that. I'd long since seen the
uselessness of condemning people for not believing. "No
man can come to me except the Father who hath sent me
draw him" (John 6:44), I reminded Claudine—and myself.

In less than an hour, the chief doctor was back, still looking puzzled, but smiling this time.

"You know, we *can't* understand what has happened to
you, Miss Golbeck," he said, apologetically. "Medical science simply has no answer for it. It doesn't fit at all into
what we know about these things. But there are some things
we *do* understand," he went on. "For instance, what has happened to you is something I could never have made happen
in a million years, but I *do* know how to fix your feet—if you
will let me." He explained something about atrophy from
disuse, ligaments, tendons, muscles, and arthritic adhesions.

"If you start walking on your feet the way they are now,"
he said, "you'll have a lot of trouble. But surgery could
straighten your feet. We could put them into walking casts
until they are strong enough to be used alone again. It's a
relatively simple procedure, one we do all the time, with
considerable success." He paused, waiting for my decision.

I was praying under my breath, asking the Lord for *His*
decision.

"Should I let him operate, Lord?" I didn't dare do anything without His permission. The poor doctor probably

thought I was talking to myself, but in a minute I had my answer. The Lord seemed to be saying, "Yes, allow him to do it. It will give you greater opportunity to witness to him about what *I* have done that he knows he could never do."

"I'll be *happy* to have you fix my feet, doctor," I said, completely satisfied with the Lord's plan in it. "It will be good to have them as well as the rest of me."

The surgery was performed the next morning while I lay flat on my back on the operating table. There was local anesthesia in my feet and ankles while the doctor manipulated them to break the adhesions and set them straight. Then, so everything would knit itself back correctly, my feet and legs were put in walking casts as high as knee stockings. But they didn't cramp my style a bit. As a matter of fact, they helped it. I needed their weight to hold me down.

I saw at once the wisdom of God's plan. I knew He could have made my feet and ankles just as suddenly well as all of my other joints, but if He had, the hospital would have seen the last of me. I'd have gone racing out into the middle of Toronto to stand on the corner of Young and Queen Streets, shouting as hard as I could, "Look at me! Look at me!" telling everyone about my miracle.

But there were some other things that needed to happen first. For one thing, I needed to get built up a little. I weighed only sixty-two pounds, hardly enough weight to hold me to the ground with my spirit soaring so.

For another thing, I looked absolutely dreadful. People wouldn't have listened to me, they'd have locked me up in some looney bin. And I might have been so intent on doing my own thing, my way, that I'd never have listened for God's plan in the midst of it all. I was just bursting to get out, to do this, to do that, and tell everybody how wonderful the Lord was, how true He was to His promises when we tried them. But first He gave me days and weeks of learning to walk in my casts, glorious days.

How wonderful it was to be able to sit up in a chair and open my own exciting mail that first week. There were precious letters from faithful friends who had held prayer services for me at eight o'clock that Saturday night. Some of them had not yet heard the news. Nonetheless, they were brimming with faith.

One wrote:

> My dearest Kay—I was with you in thought and prayer last night at eight o'clock, and felt most happy about it. The text for my evening devotion was, "If the Spirit of him that raised up Jesus from the dead dwell in you, he that raised up Christ from the dead shall also quicken your mortal bodies by his Spirit that dwelleth in you" (Romans 8:11). I felt it was very wonderful that that verse should have been on May 6, the evening portion, and I claimed it for you.

Did ever anyone have such faith-filled friends as I?

Two days after my miracle, Mr. McDermott came for a visit. What a look of wonderment and then joy was on his face when he saw my empty bed, and then me—dressed in my blue bathrobe, sitting up in a chair. Tears streamed down as he knelt beside me and prayed his thanksgiving for God's mercy. Then with the help of a crutch and a cane, I walked across the room for him. Before he left that day, he prayed again, reaffirming his Saturday night prayer, rebuking the disease and saying, "Lord, we await the carrying out of Your healing grace to every cell of this body."

After the news had gotten around, the mail was laden with new rejoicings at the wonderful works of God. One dear friend extended a special invitation:

> Oh, my dear, how glad we are to have your letter and to know that your faith and ours is being confirmed (or *rewarded* is better). I always feel guilty when something wonderful like your recovery takes place. . . . It took more

prayers than I have said to bring it about. Sometimes my only comfort is the line, "Prayer is the soul's sincere desire, unuttered or expressed. . . ." When will you be able to leave the hospital? We want to borrow a car and come for you. You have always said that you wouldn't come until you could help me. If you could only imagine what an angel of mercy you would seem if you could come and sit in the garden with the babies while I finish my housecleaning. . . .

The thought that I might again be of some use to somebody was too beautiful to contemplate. But the letter went on to remind me that Saint Paul had a very long wait after his Damascus vision before he was sent out for his big work. My friend counseled me not to be disappointed if God didn't make my new work known to me immediately. "Rest in faith," she wrote, "that God has saved you for some purpose, and in His own good time, He will show that purpose to you."

During the next few weeks, everyone I knew came to see me. As each one came in the door, I'd greet him with an urgent, "I'm so *glad* to see you! But would you mind, please, before you sit down—would you go to the coffee shop and get me something to eat? I'm just starving!" They might raise their eyebrows at me, knowing I had finished my lunch only half an hour before, but they'd go and bring me a hot-dog or something, and we'd visit while I stuffed myself. I ate everything, and everything agreed with me. In my desire to get some flesh on my bones, I was more of a bottomless pit than the boys at the mission had been. But I got results I never saw on them. In one month, I gained forty pounds!

That the weight gain made a vast difference in my appearance came home to me one day when a nurse who had been on vacation during the time of my miracle came into the room to take my temperature, feel my pulse, and record them on the chart.

"Whatever happened to that poor old lady who was in this bed?" she asked.

"What old lady?" I asked, knowing no one else had been in that bed for years.

"Oh, I don't remember her name," the nurse said, "because I hadn't been working here very long before I was gone for a month, and this isn't my floor. But one day I was called to help give the poor old soul a blood transfusion. We had to do a cutdown on her ankle, and she was in such misery, I got simply furious with the doctors, really storming at them for not letting the poor old lady die. She was practically dead already, and I didn't see any sense in torturing her."

By then, I could contain myself no longer.

"That poor old lady's me," I told her. "And I don't think I'm going to die for a little while yet. It looks as if God has other plans for me, and I'm getting well instead."

On the first day of my miracle, the nurses had put me in a wheelchair to roll me down the hall. When one of them asked me where I'd like to go first, I didn't hesitate for a moment. You wouldn't either if you'd been lying on your face for over two years, enduring the indignities of a bedpan in that position.

"To the bathroom," I said, laughing, but meaning every word of it. At my request, the nurse shut me into the little cubicle all by myself for just a few moments. It was so wonderful . . . I just closed my eyes, and with tears streaming down, from my very private if rather undignified throne, I sang, "Praise God from whom all blessings flow . . . "

I had never sung anything with a more abundant heart.

16

Lady Liberty

On June 9, 1944, at the end of a gloriously ravenous month, I was discharged from the hospital and went to stay with friends. Mother was eager for me to stay with her, but the area in which she was living was so damp, the doctors told me I couldn't risk living there. My creaky bones and joints had been restored to some degree of usefulness already, my muscles reactivated, and I was walking under my own steam, with only one crutch and a cane to help me. My walking casts provided just enough ballast to keep me from soaring off somewhere into the heavenlies.

Everywhere I went, praising God, people looked at me as if they thought I was crazy. And they were right. I *was* crazy—crazy with the joy of being set free by the goodness of God's love to me. I wanted to walk everywhere, and I wanted to tell everybody. It was such a marvelous world outdoors—couldn't they see it?

There was so much sky! I had forgotten how big a tree was, how many apples could grow on one limb without breaking it, how the grapes formed such symmetrical clusters. Roses in florists' vases in hospital rooms didn't look anything like roses twining around blue delphinium stalks in someone's yard. Every shrub, every blade of grass, each tiny flower amazed me with its color and beauty.

And the nights! I had forgotten the vastness of the dark blue velvet quilt all tied down with stars, and the silver path our lady moon spreads on the rippling waters.

I was ecstatic with delight to hear the breathtaking rapture of the woodthrush singing in the twilight, its song not filtered through window screens and walls. There was so much to see, so much to hear. And as the year rolled on, I couldn't believe that autumn had ever been that brilliant before. Had the reds and golds of maples always been so vivid? The leaves danced so merrily down? I wondered why they dressed so gaily just to die.

And I wondered, too, at some things that were not joy to me.

To my utter dismay, not everyone to whom I told the story of God's mercy was able to believe it. Their eyes would glance toward my cane and casts as if they felt sorry for me. How could they—when I was the happiest person in the world, the most blessed of all His creation?

When I gave my testimony of joy in the mother church of the little mission where I first encountered the love of Jesus, and where they had been praying for my healing for years, they just sat there in dead, stony silence. Not one of them believed or rejoiced with me. They just couldn't accept that the Lord was my healer in such a supernatural way. They thought that miracles had stopped in the Book of Acts, and I sensed that they'd have been happier to see me in my bed of pain again than to face the awesome reality of God's power.

But not even that kind of rejection could dampen my own rejoicing and exuberance for long. And there were some who did not reject what God had done for me but wrote letters or came to see me, wondering how they or their loved ones might receive miracles of God's healing themselves. Seeking God's wisdom in how to counsel them, I was wonderfully helped by a letter from my "radio pastor," the Reverend James Finlay. Through the years, I had been blessed to hear his Sunday morning sermons over the radio while I was in the hospital ward. A friend of mine was in his congregation at the Carlton Street United Church, known as the House of Friendship. At her request, he had come to visit me, and occasional correspondence had passed between us during the years. This time he wrote,

> What shall we say to all who will come to you with great hunger of soul, longing to enter into your experience of physical healing? . . .
>
> It seems to me the thing we are compelled to say is what I have felt about your own inner attitude. Longing as you did to be physically well, physical well-being was never the major objective of your yearnings. The great desire of your heart was to be so equipped in every way that you would be the most usable to God anywhere and everywhere that He might want you. If that involved restoration to physical well-being, then so let it be. If, not because God wills physical illness, but because He can and does use it mightily—if through that you could be the most potent force in His hand, then your attitude has been, as I have known you, so let it be. . . .
>
> As your colleagues in pain write to you and as you visit them, you must be able to discern in some measure what is the note of appeal in their hearts. It must never be for healing alone, but for healing incidental to something much greater. . . . We do not limit God, neither do we predict precisely what He will do with any one of us.
>
> All we know is that if we yield ourselves to Him completely, whatever is our lot can be the channel of the expression of the essence of His Spirit to our fellows. . . .

In the midst of all the glad freedom of sharing and going and doing, I had my ear tuned to the Father, asking Him all the time, "What are You going to do with me now, Lord? You said You had a work for me to do. Where is it? Am I almost ready to begin?"

I'd always loved children. As a teenager, I'd decided to have fifteen or so when I got married, but at eighteen, I learned from our family doctor that the Lord hadn't made me for bearing children of my own. Maybe now He was going to let me be the matron of an orphanage—

But the next step, as it turned out, was nothing so logical as all that. As a matter of fact, the next step was so unbelievable, so crazy, that I couldn't have agreed to it if He had told me that far ahead of time. Just set free from virtual imprisonment in a hospital for eight and a half years, I wouldn't have believed that He was about to send me to a real prison, the kind with bars on the windows, for an even longer stretch.

But first there was an interlude of freedom, a whole year of learning to live and walk again.

About three weeks after my miracle, I was sitting in an armchair in my room one morning, craning my neck to marvel over every inch of sky I could see out the high windows. My feet, in their walking casts, were resting lightly on the floor. It was such a marvelous day! And suddenly I heard something that was going to make it more marvelous still—footsteps coming down the hallway toward my room. I had long ago learned to recognize the footsteps of all the hospital staff, and there was no mistaking the owner of *these* footsteps. They had to belong to my beloved Dr. Ferrier, who had been out of the country again during the miracle of my healing. I knew that his trips to Europe with his wife were not frivolous vacations. They were earnest pilgrimages to try to find the grave of their son, a pilot in the war, who had been declared "missing in action."

When Dr. Ferrier walked in the door, my heart was racing. Had they found the grave this time? And what would *he* have to say about what had happened to me? He said nothing at first, just stood and looked at me for a long moment while his careworn face nearly fell apart with astonishment —and joy.

Then, "This just has to be God!" he exclaimed, raising his hands into the air. "There's no other possible explanation. Apart from God, it just couldn't have happened. And they tell me you can even walk. Is that—can that really be true, Kay? Walking, after all these years?"

For answer, I stood up and went slowly toward him. We shook hands almost reverently, and when he had let me go, I walked back and forth several times across the little room. He was full of rejoicing at every step.

Afterward, we had a wonderful visit, a time when he shared my joy at my healing and when I expressed my sympathy that he had not been able to locate his son's grave.

"It's all right, Kay," he said gently. "It's all right. My son isn't in a grave—not really."

He sat with his head bowed with grief for only a moment, then shook it as if to revive the happy memories of his son's life.

"But let's get back to you, Kay. What God has done for you is beyond anything I could have expected. Now I want to give you some advice."

I couldn't resist teasing him just a little. "Are you going to prepare me for the worst again, Dr. Ferrier?" I asked him, reminding him of his pessimism over the years, his dire prognosis of my ailments—that I'd have to quit work or never be able to work again, that I was a sixteen-cylinder motor in a four-cylinder chassis . . . He laughed with me at the memories, then turned serious again.

"No, Kay, this time I'm not preparing you for the worst

144

—but for enjoying and holding onto the best that God has seen fit to give you. First of all, I want you to promise me that you'll start eating a real breakfast every day. No more, just orange juice and coffee. That's the quickest way in the world for you to get run down."

I nodded my head, aware that God was speaking to me through him. Then I waited for his second instruction.

"Next, you must get out of our Canadian winter and stay out of it for a couple of years at least."

"Oh, but I couldn't leave Canada."

He looked at me with a no-nonsense sternness: "You've had a miracle from God, young lady. Don't tempt Providence by staying through our winters until you're thoroughly built up and all this sickness is completely out of your system."

"But where could I go? I don't have the slightest idea of any place to stay, any work I could do in the United States . . ."

"I don't know either," he said, "but surely God will provide you with something."

As we said goodbye, a lump came up in my throat, and there were tears in his eyes. He'd been such a kind friend through the years. He shook my hand again, saying brusquely, "It's set me up for a year just to see you walking, Kay. Take care of yourself, and promise you'll come to see me every year."

With that, he was gone, and I sat and listened to his footsteps echoing down the creaky old corridor. "Where's he going next?" I wondered aloud, hoping he was on his way to deliver a baby. From things I'd heard, there must have been hundreds of babies named for him along the Lakeshore Road. Dr. Ferrier never refused to make a house call, no matter the weather or the time of night. And he almost had to be reminded to send bills for his services. It was the patient he was always thinking about.

Years later, when Dr. Ferrier's long and fruitful life was

finished, he didn't have to retire or get sick to leave for heaven. He just dropped out of this world and into the next one day on the sidewalk—on his way to make a house call. What a joyful reunion he must have had with his son then.

I resolved to take Dr. Ferrier's advice about eating a good breakfast every day, but how in the world could I even begin to think about leaving Canada's winters to live in the United States? How could I even afford to go there, much less make a living for myself once I had arrived? There was simply no way—unless the Lord provided it.

A week later, my sister Edith, who lived in Royal Oak, Michigan, with her husband and two children, invited me to come for a visit. Her children were eager to meet their strange auntie who did such funny things as get up and walk when she was supposed to be an invalid the rest of her life. Edith sent me a train ticket, and I set out, with two casts and two canes. Michigan would hardly qualify as the sunny south, but at least it represented a step in the right direction.

All the while, I knew that this was a temporary sojourning, and that God's special work for me would be revealed as soon as I was strong enough to tackle it. Meanwhile, I kept on going to as many places and doing as many things as my finances and ever-growing strength would allow. As each experience was accomplished, I crossed it off in my little red notebook.

While I was still staying with friends in Toronto, I had received a letter from a good friend, Dorothy Campbell. I hadn't seen her in years. She said she was going to Pendle Hill, near Philadelphia, Pennsylvania, to take a course or two, and she would like me to visit her there.

I replied, telling her without specific explanation that I could not go to Pendle Hill just then. I didn't want to come right out and say that I couldn't afford the trip.

After I arrived at Edith's, Dorothy bombarded me with a telegram, a special-delivery letter, and then a night letter repeating her invitation. I couldn't ignore such a battery of attention.

"Lord, are You trying to tell me something?" When I didn't hear a direct answer, I put out a fleece: "The only way I'll know that this is Your plan is if You provide the money for a train ticket, Lord."

Edith held a tea for me a few days later, and I enjoyed being the guest of honor. After the women had gone home, I helped Edith wash the dishes and clear the things away, finding great joy in being able to do these little things to help. As I took the linen cloth off her dining table to fold it and put it away in the buffet, I found a small envelope underneath one corner of it. "To your sister" was the address on the outside.

I took it to Edith and asked her what it meant.

"Go ahead and open it, Kay. Don't you have any curiosity?"

"Too much, probably," I admitted. "But I like to think about what might be in such a message before I read it and also to pray that God will show me what He means by it."

I opened the envelope and read the small note aloud:

Dear Kay—I just wanted to leave a little gift for you. I trust you will find it useful. Love, a friend in the Lord.

There was no other signature, and I understood why the envelope had been hidden under the tablecloth instead of being handed to me. There were some bills enclosed. I counted them out—just exactly what I needed for the train ticket to Pendle Hill. And so I knew I was to go.

I boarded the 11:30 night train from Detroit to Pittsburgh on May 1, not quite a year from the day I was anointed with oil. I was so excited, my berth was almost

147

a waste of money, because I couldn't sleep. It was so fascinating to lie there, watching the city, then the countryside, scoot by out of the sooty window. Finally though, the rhythmic chugging of the engine lulled me off, and I slept soundly to awaken just in time to get dressed for my change of trains in Pittsburgh.

I boarded the train for Philadelphia, happy to be making part of my trip in daylight. For an hour or so out of Pittsburgh the tremendous industries along the way held their own fascination for me. Then suddenly we were in rolling hills, going around curves so long that I could see both ends of the train at once. At Johnstown I was awed by eight miles of the Bethlehem Steel Company on each side of the city, and at Altoona there was an immense horseshoe curve of great beauty. Then Harrisburg, and from there on, green grass and small farms nestling in valleys made a countryside of indescribable beauty and peace.

It was dark again when we arrived in the City of Brotherly Love, but I could feel the throbbing of a big metropolis. By the time I had completed the last lap of my journey, taking a cab to Pendle Hill, I felt like a seasoned traveler.

Pendle Hill was an estate of eight acres or so. There was a great stone house set in the midst of a spreading lawn of truly majestic trees. The upstairs of the house had several large dormitory rooms, and a few apartments for married couples and their children. A big downstairs dining room was used for lectures, and there were two kitchens, a sitting room, living room, and library, as well as a terrace for tea on fine days. Other stone buildings on the campus had various functions, one of them being the home of Howard and Anna Brinton, directors of Pendle Hill.

Officially, Pendle Hill was designated as the Quaker Religious and Social Center. Everything about it had the austere simplicity characteristic of Quaker establishments. Dr. Sollman, formerly editor of a Berlin newspaper and one of Pendle Hill's resident lecturers, described it with a twinkle in his eye as a "place where queer people live, work, and study together, and learn not to quarrel." Although it was in part an "academic" community, the priority was always on learning to live.

Dorothy and I renewed our acquaintance, and then I threw myself into the fascination of studying under really competent teachers. I reviewed my French under Madame Sheffer, a beautiful Swiss woman; took part with Jews, Gentiles, Atheists, Protestants, Catholics, Orientals, and others in discussing the teachings of Jesus; sat enthralled as Douglas Steere, professor from Haverford College, lectured on Thomas à Kempis' *Imitation of Christ,* St. Frances de Sales, and von Hugel.

I was greedy to hear everything. Miraculously, nothing seemed too difficult for me to grasp. And there was far more than the excitement of learning. There were faculty children to watch at play and to love. There was excitement in corporate worship. And in silence and solitude. Exactly everything I needed for the restoration to wholeness of my mind and spirit while my body recovered full health and strength.

On the campus, I found my own private sanctuary, a small clearing in the center of a grove of the magnificent trees. I sensed at once that it would be holy ground for me, and I asked God to be with me there while I poured out my innermost thoughts to Him. One day I glimpsed the glory of perfect fellowship with the heavenly Father. As I rejoiced and gave thanks, there were wildly exuberant bursts of music from low branches right over my head. Half a dozen mockingbirds presented a perfect symphony on limbs so low I could have stretched out my hands and touched them. Four other unidentified songsters came and rested on the end of the log where I sat, the air throbbing with such rapturous song that my heart overflowed. Then a squirrel joined us, followed by her furry babies. These little creatures of God surrounded me, apparently without fear. We were all sensing His perfect love.

Was ever a living being so blessed as I, surrounded by His perfect creatures, all praising Him? I was praising Him out loud, too, at first in English words, but my hallelujahs soon crescendoed into ecstatic utterances that I didn't understand. I knew instinctively that the beautifully melodic syllables that poured so effortlessly off my tongue, like water babbling over smooth stones, were sounds of perfect praise to my King.

All that marvelous day, the air was vibrant for me with the carolings of orioles, cardinals, robins, song sparrows, thrushes, red-eyed vireos, and several other birds I had never heard before. The hedges were ablaze with mountain laurel and rhododendron. Wisteria hung like pale veils, all lavender and misty white, from the perfect green trees. Roses, azaleas, and peonies like great pink dinner plates nodding their heads in approval of the perfect pattern of everything, blended their individual uniqueness together in a paean of praise to the Creator of it all.

It was too much for one heart to hold. And always there was more. And more. I marveled that I could hold so much joy and not explode.

I had been at Pendle Hill two weeks, studying, resting, soaking up knowledge, refreshment, and blessing like a dried sponge in a pail of life-giving water. It was all so wonderful that I went down on my knees beside my bed one afternoon, just thanking the Lord for letting me be there.

"Oh, Lord, this is so marvelous!" I told Him. "If there were only some way I could earn my keep and stay on for a while, I'd be *so* grateful. I just can't get enough of learning. My mind has been rusty; I've been out of touch for so long —I *so* wish I could stay—"

There was a lot more I wanted to tell Him, but I heard a knock on my door. "Come in!" I called out, being still a little bit slow in getting up off my knees.

The door opened and in walked Anna Brinton, co-director of the school. In typical Quaker fashion, she said, "Katherine Golbeck, I understand that you can type."

"Well," I replied, "I used to do secretarial work, but I haven't touched a typewriter for years."

"That's all right," she assured me. "A skill like that isn't ever lost—it can always be limbered up again. I'm desperately in need of some help just now. Would you do me the great favor of staying on as my personal secretary?"

I hesitated, too overcome with emotion to speak for a moment, and she must have taken the delay to mean that I might refuse her offer.

"I've figured it all out," she said. "Four hours a day, six days a week, would cover your full expense of being here. And we'd be glad to pay you eighty cents an hour for any additional work we might ask you to do."

I could not hold back the tears.

"Oh, Anna Brinton, how good our God is to me. You saw where I was when you came in. I was just asking the Father if He would provide a way for me to stay in this wonderful place. My board is paid for two more days, but after that, I was going to have to leave. I don't know if I *can* earn my keep, but if you're willing to let me try, I'll be in heaven—"

How much limbering up of my secretarial skills there was to be done! I checked a shorthand book out of the campus library that afternoon, and when everything in it seemed more Greek than English to me, I put it under my pillow and went to sleep, praying that the Lord would bring to my remembrance everything I needed to know about it. I felt that was stretching the scripture of John 14:26 a bit, but He had provided the opportunity, so He would have to be able to make me fit it.

The next day in the chapel we heard a lecture by a man from India. I practiced by taking shorthand notes on all he said. When I had transcribed my notes, I got up my nerve to ask him to look the transcript over, explaining why I was

151

trying to upgrade my note-taking skills. Glory to God! The only things I had missed were the names of a few Indian officials and two of the villages he mentioned. It looked as if I was all set to be a "career girl" as well as a student for a while.

By the end of June, I scarcely recognized myself in the mirror. I weighed 122 pounds and looked the picture of health, enjoying to the full the crowds of young people who came for conferences on many weekends. As a matter of fact, even though I didn't participate in their ballgames, I felt almost like one of them. I had become impatient occasionally with what I called the "old maid" types who sometimes used the extra bed in my room. I had to chuckle at my indignation about their rigid ideas about beds, windows, doors, and everything else having to be just so for their comfort. It had been such a short time ago that I couldn't even stand to have anyone walk across the floor of my room, let alone share one with me. What a transformation there had been!

Before the end of June, Dorothy and I took a train for Plainfield, New Jersey, where we stopped with friends before fulfilling one of the most important dreams in my little red notebook: I was going to see New York City! I knew somehow that this visit was to have a special significance.

Dorothy was having a bad spell of asthma on the day we planned to go into the city, so I set out with two young girls who were eager to do some sightseeing. We started from Plainfield by train, then took a ferry to the south end of New York and a subway to the Battery. From there, another ferry ride as my mind was boggled by all my eyes could take in —the great warehouses along the Hudson, the immense bridges, a big hospital ship, Governor's Island, Ellis Island, and then, right in front of me, the great Lady Liberty herself.

The Statue of Liberty was much bigger than I thought she would be, standing on a tremendous pedestal. An elevator took us up 150 feet to the foot of the statue where we looked at the view from a balcony. I walked all around, debating with myself: Should I climb to the top? I knew there were twelve more stories, 168 narrow winding steps. Dare I try it? Thinking about how only a little more than a year earlier such a thing would have been beyond my contemplation, I felt I *must* do it now, as a kind of thank offering to my King, a sacrifice of praise.

Step after step after step—it was a long way, hard work, but also one of the most exciting adventures of my life. And I made it!

While I paused to catch my breath, my mind flashed back to the day when young Doctor Cornett had come into my hospital room and said, "You'll never walk again." Such rejoicing surged through the inside of me that I had to express it on the outside, no matter who was looking on, no matter what anybody might think. I stood right in the middle window of the crown of Lady Liberty, my eyes swimming before the panorama spread in front of me, my whole being exulting in the fresh breeze. Taking a deep, deep breath, I sang, not quietly and carefully, but as loud as I could, so all the world could hear:

> Praise God from whom all blessings flow (especially right now, *this* blessing, Lord); Praise Him all creatures here below (every creature, great and small); Praise Him above ye heavenly hosts (I could hear all heaven rejoicing with me!); Praise Father, Son and Holy Ghost!

My spirit overflowed with hallelujahs. I had never felt more free of self. Everything in me wanted to shout, "Come on, everybody! Let's all praise God!" Oh, I felt so wonderful, whether the people looking at me so queerly understood it or not.

One of the persons who *did* understand, completely, was my radio pastor. When I wrote the Reverend James Finlay

153

later, telling him about my climb to the top of Liberty, he wept for joy. In his reply, he wrote,

> I cannot imagine anything more faith-strengthening than to know that you, Kay Golbeck, have actually stood at the top of the Statue of Liberty, commanding such a height by the grace of God and your own spirit of cooperation with His will. The top of the Statue of Liberty! "If the Son shall make you free, you shall be free indeed."

I *was* free indeed. The shackles of illness that had bound my feet for so long had been broken by the power of the mighty God.

The next day I didn't feel tired at all! And I had the strange sensation that I was ready for the new work. More importantly, God had done so many wonderful new things for me and through me that I was sure that regardless of what the new work might be, God could handle it all.

Epilogue

GOD HAD MADE KAY GOLBECK ready to do a new work for Him. Within a few weeks of her climb to the top of the Statue of Liberty, the Lord called her to minister as a chaplain at the penitentiary for women near Goochland, Virginia. There, for more than eight years, she served as His instrument for unlocking hardened hearts to His love, for setting captives free. Then Kay became critically ill again, this time with a killer known as myasthenia gravis. When it had reduced her to a terribly weakened condition, friends came from New Brunswick to take her home to die.

But the indomitable Kay Golbeck didn't die; she kept on trusting God to heal her. And He did, very gradually this time, as she was obedient to His vision of yet another new work for Him. By a series of remarkable events, Kay Golbeck became the founder of Singing Waters, an internationally known retreat center near Orangeville, Canada. There, God is still working through her, continuing to answer the first real prayer of her life, "Oh, dear Lord, please don't ever let our relationship become ordinary." He's answering another of her prayers, too, that no one who comes to Singing Waters will go away without a song in his heart. And every day, there is some wonderful new thing to be learned about God.